W9-BVJ-599

THE EVANGELICAL HISTORIANS

The Historiography of George Marsden, Nathan Hatch, and Mark Noll

Maxie B. Burch

University Press of America, Inc.
Lanham • New York • London

Copyright © 1996 by
University Press of America,® Inc.
4720 Boston Way
Lanham, Maryland 20706

3 Henrietta Street
London, WC2E 8LU England

Library of Congress Cataloging-in-Publication Data

Burch, Maxie B.
The Evangelical historians : the historiography of George Marsden,
Nathan Hatch, and Mark Noll / Maxie B. Burch.
p.   cm.
Includes bibliographical references and index.
1. Church historians--United States--Biography. 2. Marsden, George
M. 3. Hatch, Nathan O. 4. Noll, Mark A. 5. North America--
Religion--History--Historiography. 6. Evangelicalism--History--20th
century--Historiography. I. Title.
BR 138.B77   1996   270'.92'273--dc20   95-43830 CIP

ISBN 0-7618-0179-0 (cloth: alk: ppr.)

⊖™The paper used in this publication meets the minimum
requirements of American National Standard for information
Sciences—Permanence of Paper for Printed Library Materials,
ANSI Z39.48—1984

Contents

93832

Preface

Among historians it is recognized as a general rule of thumb that when writing about the work other historians it is safest to chose those who are either dead or retired because they are less likely to change their minds. This book is a departure from this general rule. The historians whose lives and scholarship are the focus of this story were chosen because they represent a significant coterie of evangelicals who are unapologetically writing history with a confessional yet rigorously professional approach. Their openly confessional approach is a unique characteristic of this block of historians, but it is their practice of networking other historians of like mind and the close personal friendships and cooperative efforts that have resulted which perhaps truly sets them apart. In other words, in addition to being historians, they are interesting people and I embarked upon this project because I was curious about who they were and what they were doing.

Over the past ten years these men have emerged as leaders in the field of American Christianity while also making significant inroads in the discussion surrounding the purpose and mission of the modern university. They write primarily about the Protestant evangelical experience in America focusing their research upon the cultural and ideological factors that shaped this experience while addressing the biblical and theological traditions that define and inform the evangelical community as well. At times they have employed history as a means of providing penetrating critiques of evangelicalism in an attempt to create a productive discussion, but they have not always been successful.

This book was written primarily with the community of historians and other interested scholars in mind, but perhaps those who share an interest in the story of Christianity in America, and particularly the Protestant evangelical experience that helped shape that story, will find this narrative of interest as well. Because the central figures are living, productive scholars, this story is still being written, but it is hoped that those who read this portion will be captured by the kind of curiosity that makes history such an intriguing pursuit.

The initial chapter is designed to provide the reader with the opportunity to meet George Marsden, Nathan Hatch, and Mark Noll by offering a brief but revealing look at their backgrounds and early experiences. The second chapter focuses on the people, ideas, and decisions that shaped their historical perspective and careers. By examining areas of conflict that have risen due to their research, chapter three offers a clear example of the kinds of issues and concerns that drive these men's scholarship. In chapter four Marsden, Hatch, and Noll speak out about the state of the modern university system, and the plight of evangelical scholarship as it struggles for respect and recognition in academic circles. This chapter also examines the institute which these men helped to create in order to further their aims of strengthening evangelical scholarship. The final chapter questions the possible lasting influence these historians will have on their discipline.

The fact that this book was completed is due to the efforts of many people who contributed to it on a variety of levels. I am indebted first of all to the historians who are its subject because without their kind cooperation and assistance at crucial junctures it would still be just an idea. I am especially grateful to Mark Noll for allowing me access to potentially sensitive materials and trusting me to use them responsibly. Bill Pitts provided direction and encouragement, and he wins the award for returning corrected chapters in what can only be referred to as "light speed." Chris Mitchell is the colleague and friend who unknowingly introduced me to these historians long before I knew them, and he is a wizard at asking penetrating questions about a project. Thanks go to Michael Russo and Steve Wells for laboring with me over the formatting and other details of which I was and am still ignorant. The motivation for this book came from my family who supported me throughout, and especially my wife and best friend, Lisa.

M. B. B.
Waco, Texas
August 24, 1995

1

A Historian's History

On April 15 and 16 of 1977, Trinity College in Deerfield, Illinois hosted a conference exploring the relationship between religion and politics during the American Revolution. The title of the conference was, "The American Revolution, The American Christian, and American Civil Religion." Trinity College Student Association sponsored the conference with this statement of purpose:

> In sponsoring such a conference, the Association seeks to perform a service for Christian scholarship in general, and to advance the scholarly work of evangelical historians on American history in particular. It is to be expected that such a conference will be of interest and benefit to both the Trinity College learning community and the public at large.[1]

The importance of this conference held in the Spring of 1977 extends beyond its subject matter. Its primary importance can be traced to the participants, the relationships these participants formed just prior to and during the conference, and the subsequent cohort of evangelical historians that emerged from this conference with the intent of maintaining their new found friendships and nurturing common interests.

Mark Noll initiated this conference while in his second year as Assistant Professor of History at Trinity College. During the Fall he met George Marsden, a visiting professor of Church History at Trinity Divinity School. Noll was already familiar with Marsden's work. He had previously read Marsden's book on the Presbyterians and wrote a review of John Woodbridge's and David Wells' book on evangelicals in which he praised Marsden's essay as the best in the book. By the time of their meeting in the Fall of 1976 they at least shared a mutual admiration for one another that only an author and a complimentary reviewer can appreciate. Over the next several months they met regularly for coffee with other members of the faculty, a time which Noll refers to as his "real graduate education."[2]

During Marsden's time at Trinity Noll used this conference as an opportunity to contact other evangelical historians he had either heard about or with whom he had corresponded. While finishing his dissertation at Vanderbilt Noll had written Nathan Hatch. Both men graduated from Wheaton in 1968 but never really knew each other as undergraduates. Hatch had written an article in 1974 which appeared in the *William and Mary Quarterly*, and, after reading the article, Noll started a correspondence with Hatch that continued over the years. So in the Spring of 1977, Noll invited Nathan Hatch, a professor of history at Notre Dame, and Harry Stout a history professor at the University of Connecticut, to give papers at the Trinity conference. Noll had heard about Stout from Marsden who taught Stout while at Calvin College. These four—George Marsden, Mark Noll, Nathan Hatch, and Harry Stout, along with Rockney McCarthey—comprised the speakers at the conference.[3]

This conference was designed to be a one time affair with no long range goals or plans for the future. The administration of Trinity approved the idea for the conference while the student association provided the money and sponsorship. The result was that everyone who participated enjoyed themselves. Good papers and lively discussion ensued and all involved agreed that it would be fun to do again. After the last session of the conference these four historians gathered at a restaurant in Deerfield over coffee to discuss other areas of interest and concern. Their conversation eventually worked around to a mutual dissatisfaction over the kind of recent scholarship that was being done on the Bible in evangelical circles—scholarship that appeared to some as not truly historical. At this point it was suggested that a conference on the historical and cultural use of the Bible in America would be a good idea. Nathan Hatch suggested that money could be available for a conference through contacts he had with a charitable foundation, and that he would look into a proposal for funding such a conference.[4] And so, what started as a one time conference on religion and politics initiated the beginnings of a network of evangelical historians with similar interests and concerns.

The circumstances and experiences that led these men from diverse backgrounds to yoke themselves together around similar commitments, interests, and beliefs to form an influential network of evangelical historians committed to rigorous historical research and the importance of integrating faith and scholarship forms one of the central themes of this book. Issues of historical methodology, research content, and academic goals will also be discussed as they apply to the three historians who are the subject of this book. Mark A. Noll, George M. Marsden, and Nathan O. Hatch were chosen as the central figures for this study because they represent the acknowledged leadership of this growing network of evangelical historians. One of the more interesting aspects of this particular network of evangelical historians is that it is characterized by close personal friendships as well as cooperative academic efforts. Over the last fifteen years, their commitment to careful and rigorous scholarship has won them acclaim in the more secular historical guild as well as among many in the evangelical world.

Who are these historians? Nathan Hatch was the 1991-92 President of the American Society of Church History. His publication, *The Democratization of American Christianity*, won the 1988 Albert C. Outler Prize in Ecumenical Church History and the Society for Historians of the Early American Republic 1989 Book Prize. In addition, he serves as the Vice-President for Graduate Studies and Research at the University of Notre Dame. George Marsden was the 1992-93 President of the American Society of Church History. He is the Francis A. McAnaney Professor of History at the University of Notre Dame, and is recognized as a leading expert on the history of Fundamentalism in America. Mark Noll holds the chair of the McManis Professor of Christian Thought at Wheaton College and is the Senior Director for the Institute for the Study of American Evangelicals located at Wheaton College.[5] A unique ability to bridge the often wide gap between professional academics and confessional beliefs is a self-conscious trait of these historians. This trait along with their rigorous scholarship and academic credentials sets them apart as a consequential block of evangelical scholars.

Personal Background

An investigation of these men's past reveals very different backgrounds, but also a common thread that seems to run through all of their early experiences. They are all heirs to a conservative Protestant upbringing. This heritage varied in degree of conservatism from moderately conservative to strongly dogmatic but all three men spoke in some form or fashion of remembering a "fundamentalist" home. The use of fundamentalist with a small "f" is intentional because, of the three men, only George Marsden came from a home in which a Fundamentalist/ Modernist controversy of a strict denominational sort permeated his family's way of life.

Mark Noll recalled being raised in a Conservative Baptist home in Iowa. He referred to it as "a normal fundamentalist home," but immediately qualified his statement by saying that he never remembered the word fundamentalism being used. He could only remember two controversies from his childhood. One controversy revolved around some people pulling out of the church in Wheaton, Illinois where his father served as Chairman of Deacons over the issue of denominational affiliation. The other controversy concerned slanderous attacks by some people in Minnesota against the pastor of the Conservative Baptist church the Nolls attended in Iowa. Noll could not remember any details except for the fact that "those folks up there just tended to be ornery sods."[6]

His parents were serious Christian people who attended church regularly and observed daily family devotions, an exercise Noll found painful as a boy. He now dryly admits to having reaped the harvest of his poor attitude as his children find them painful as well. Both parents were raised Methodist but later in life his father had a conversion experience due to a caring Baptist minister and consequently became a Baptist. This experience seemed to have been influential in Noll's subsequent Conservative Baptist background.

He could not recall his parents ever speaking expressly about the importance of developing the intellect as a Christian duty but he thought they had an intuitive sense about it and therefore encouraged their children to pursue education.[7] The intuitive sense Noll described may have been due to the fact that both parents grew up during the Depression. His father was an engineer and the first in his family to finish college.

Nathan Hatch's family seemed to be closer to the crux of controversy than Noll's . He too spoke of his home as "sort of fundamentalist," but he attributed this more to growing up in the orbit of Columbia Bible College (CBC) in Columbia, South Carolina than to the nature of his home life. This was because CBC, like other bible colleges, placed a heavy emphasis on piety and conservative mores. His father was Southern Presbyterian while his mother grew up Southern Baptist.

His father's dramatic conversion experience while a senior at Duke University contributed to his later decision to attend graduate school at Columbia Bible College. There he came under the influence of the founder of the school, Robert McQuilken.[8] McQuilken had been an associate of Charles G. Trumbell after Trumbell became an advocate of Keswick Holiness teachings. As a result of this association, Columbia Bible College became an important center for promoting Keswick views.[9]

Hatch believes that this Keswick teaching had a significant influence on his father, referring to his father as "a disciple of McQuilken." It is probable that his father found Keswick teaching compatible with his Reformed background. The Keswick position on sanctification did not follow that of the Wesleyan tradition which stated one was perfected by "the Baptism of the Holy Spirit." The Keswick position held that continuing sanctification referred to the spirit's role of empowering the Christian. They spoke of this empowering as a process of continual emptying and filling for "enduing or power for service."[10] Thus they accepted the Calvinist's emphasis of total dependency on Christ and the pervasive effect of sin, while stressing at the same time the need for achieving a higher level of spirituality and service for Christ. The Keswick teaching also promoted concepts such as "resting in the Lord," "peace," and "victory." Because it did not promote dispensationalism, as did other fundamentalist groups, it proved to be a less divisive movement.[11]

Hatch's father was ordained in the Southern Presbyterian Church after finishing his Master of Divinity degree at CBC. Then upon completion of a Master Degree in Psychology at The University of Chicago in 1949 he was asked by McQuilken to join the faculty of CBC as a professor of Bible and Psychology. He taught Bible and Psychology for the next thirty-eight years. Hatch spoke of his father as being a gentle and godly man with an extremely irenic temperament, who liked to say, "If you don't have anything kind to say, keep your mouth shut." Their home was fundamentalist but "without the harsh side of fundamentalism, there was not a fundamentalist attitude. We didn't drink or dance but none of that was imposed on us in a harsh sense."[12] Perhaps the Keswick influence provided his father with a means of tempering the intensity of doctrinal issues that often swirled around fundamentalist bible schools, allowing him to focus instead on the practical issues of living out the Christian life in "peace" and "victory." Or, it may just have been that his father's natural temperament was irenic. At any rate, regardless of the religious politics that may have surrounded CBC, the controversies that often accompanied Fundamentalism were apparently not a significant influence in the Hatch home.

George Marsden was born into controversy. He described his father, Robert Marsden, as an "Old School" Presbyterian, a disciple of J. Gresham Machen, a doctrinalist, and a member of the first graduating class of Westminster Seminary. Marsden was born in Middletown, Pennsylvania where his father pastored the First Presbyterian Church. He remembered the tension in the town created by the Presbyterian schism of the 1930s. The people who ran the town were also members of the older, established Presbyterian church. The Marsden family was ostracized by these established families when his father chose to follow J. Gresham Machen out of the Presbyterian Church to affiliate with the newly formed Orthodox Presbyterian Church (O. P. C.). Part of this alienation Marsden attributed to a prevalent attitude among Orthodox Presbyterians. For Orthodox

Presbyterians, "being a Christian meant standing against the dominant culture, even other Christians. They thought of themselves as the only true Christians."[13] Marsden's childhood was permeated by both religious and cultural tensions.

The pervasiveness of this tension is illustrated by a memory his mother once shared of her wedding day in 1935. Robert Marsden had two good friends who took part in the ceremony; Carl McIntire, who served as the presiding minister at the wedding and was to later head the separatist American Council of Christian Churches, and the best man, Harold John Ockenga, who later helped found the National Association of Evangelicals. According to Marsden's mother, the three men spent the minutes just prior to the ceremony arguing over which direction the church should go. The Fundamentalist verses Modernist controversy in the Presbyterian Church had reached a boiling point by this time and choices were being made. Robert Marsden chose to follow Machen into the Orthodox Presbyterian Church. Carl McIntire followed Machen but later separated from him to form his own Bible Presbyterian Church. Ockenga chose to stay in the Presbyterian Church. The point is that Marsden did not remember either of these two former friends of his father being in the picture during his childhood. The choices the three men made essentially precluded any further friendship. The only exception Marsden recalled was a letter his father wrote to the *New York Times* in response to an article in the *Times* essentially picturing McIntire as crazy. Marsden's father wrote the *Times* saying that he had not always agreed with McIntire on every issue, but he knew McIntire was not crazy.[14]

Marsden's father later became the Missionary Secretary for the Orthodox Presbyterian Church, and Chief Executive Officer at Westminster Seminary. Marsden remembered studying the Westminster Confession of Faith in the young people's group which his father led at their church, and recalled how strict the Orthodox Presbyterians were in defining themselves confessionally. There seemed to be no separation between his father's work and beliefs, which always found him in the middle of church politics. Young Marsden's life was subsequently surrounded and influenced by controversy both within the church and outside it.[15]

He did recall a more moderating influence during his childhood. Marsden's grandmother lived with them in a large house built in the 1830s. She became an adult around the turn of the century and lived out a kind "liberal pietism," which Marsden described as having "conservative mores such as strict Sabbath observance and the like, but she liked to fish, play cards and had no objections to drinking." He believed this liberal pietism had a moderating influence on him in contrast to his more dogmatic father and passive mother.[16]

How much one's later life interests, profession, and view of life are shaped by the experiences of growing up is hard to say, and care should be taken in drawing quick conclusions to this question. But it seems apparent that these three men shared similar backgrounds based in a conservative brand of Protestantism they referred to as fundamentalist. Thus they were all able to speak of some form of fundamentalist mindset present in their homes, even if for Noll and Hatch this mindset was a more latent than militant type of fundamentalism. But the experiences of fundamentalism they shared were not experienced in a cultural vacuum. How were their family's attitudes toward Christianity and culture influential in shaping their early religious experiences, and how did these attitudes affect their future faith commitments, education choices, and career decisions?

The Early Shaping of Faith and Career
Mark Noll

During his childhood, Noll's family were conservative Baptists who lived in the urban mid-West during the 1950s and 1960s. Conservative Baptists in Iowa were a small group who kept mostly to themselves. Noll remembered his church cooperating with other evangelical churches in Cedar Rapids for an occasional crusade but not much else. The pastor of this Conservative Baptist Church in Cedar Rapids was from the William B. Riley network in Minnesota.[17] William B. Riley had been a leader of the premillennialist wing of the fundamentalist movement in the early decades of the twentieth century. He promoted a brand of fundamentalism that was revivalist, and pietist with an emphasis on moral reform.[18] Noll described the pastor of their church as a "gentle fundamentalist" who emphasized the Bible but without much in the way of exegesis.[19] This brand of fundamentalism located in a Conservative Baptist Church in Iowa was relatively free from controversy or divisiveness and must have been somewhat compelling considering Noll's future decisions regarding his confessional beliefs. The irenic spirit of his pastor and parents, the broader religious and social conservatism of Iowa, and the fundamentalist tradition that undergirded his Conservative Baptist upbringing were all essential ingredients in Noll's early life.

Noll's conservative background plus his desire to play college basketball made his decision to attend Wheaton College in 1964 a natural one. As stated before, his parents were not overt in promoting a conscious view of the need for Christians to develop a strong intellect, but neither did they have an anti-intellectual attitude. Noll did not remember his family or the people he grew up with taking education very seriously, at least not as seriously as they do today. This lack of interest may have been more a reflection of the general attitudes of his region of the country in the early 1960s than a statement about his family in particular—an observation that is supported by the fact that barely half of his high school graduating class attended college.[20]

Interestingly enough he did not major in history even though he enjoyed reading history. Instead he majored in English primarily because he liked books. Christian issues were not crucial for him at this time since books and basketball were the consuming interests of his life in college. This does not indicate, however, that he was not examining his faith in some significant ways. The moral Protestant pietism he found at Wheaton, and perhaps had experienced growing up, began to wear thin on him at this time. Noll said he did not sense an attitude of grace in the moralism of the school's tradition. He admitted, though, that this could have been as much his problem of misunderstanding their concept of grace as their failure to demonstrate it consistently. An example of this tension is found in Noll's observation that Wheaton did not seem to recognize its enshrining of a high Anglican like C. S. Lewis who was known to smoke and drink, as inconsistent with the schools fundamentalist mores and norms.[21] As he put it, "I wasn't too pleased with Evangelicalism for good and bad reasons."[22]

He spoke of being helped in his Christian pilgrimage his senior year by reading Roland Bainton's, *Here I Stand: The Life of Martin Luther.* What stood out to him in his reading of Luther was the strong emphasis on grace that permeated the story. He was further helped around this time by his future wife who introduced him to the Reformed faith. Her family belonged to an Orthodox Presbyterian Church in New Jersey and it was through this contact that he began reading the theology of Calvin and other Reformed thinkers. Noll, commenting on the discovery of the Reformed theological tradition, said, "That perspective fit with my own religious experience which is pretty Augustinian. I quite eagerly, readily, and rapidly, upon finding out about Reformed thinkers, became Reformed."[23] Due to his Baptist background he struggled some with the issue of baptism, but after reading some books on the issue he was further convinced of the Reformed position regarding the sacraments.

How did this decision fit with his early religious experience in Iowa?

It would appear that his early Conservative Baptist background provided a theological foundation not unlike that which he found in the Orthodox Presbyterian Church, though Noll did say that even now he is more of a Congregationalist in polity than a Presbyterian. Perhaps the difference between Conservative Baptists and Orthodox Presbyterians for Noll was more sociological than theological. Noll was attracted by the Reformed emphasis on sin and grace that left one free to live for Christ without the added imposition of more cultural/religious rules. "So I was very pleased to find Luther, and then soon thereafter some Presbyterians who really didn't care whether you took an occasional drink and smoked an occasional pipe, and thought it was more important to have a heart transformed by grace than a very detailed moral code in place."[24] Noll's shift from Conservative Baptist to Orthodox Presbyterian did not represent a major change in theological direction. Instead it seemed to be a move to a nicer house in the same neighborhood.

After graduating from Wheaton College in 1968, Noll decided to enter graduate school at the University of Iowa where he completed an M. A. degree in comparative literature. His work focused on the German poet Novalis, and it was during this time of study he began to realize that his real interests in literature revolved around historical, theological, and philosophical issues.[25] It is not clear how Noll's study of and conversion to a Reformed position was related to this awareness of a deepening interest in things historical, theological, and philosophical, but it appears these two aspects of his life converged at approximately the same time. It is not beyond the realm of possibility that he found the Reformed tradition to be as intellectually stimulating as it was compatible to his own religious experience.

He married Margaret Packer in 1969, and not long after that entered Trinity Evangelical Divinity School to pursue a M. A. degree in Church History. His reason for this decision seems more personal than academic or career oriented.

> And then I decided to take a year to study the history of Christianity. Although I had not studied history formally, I had always loved to read it. It seemed intuitively that were I to find a kind of faith that could be affirmed whole-heartedly, and which would grasp me whole-heartedly, it would be found in the past. I really don't know why I thought that, but it was the case, so I decided to take a year in studying church history as a kind of grounding in the Christian faith and then go on and do whatever it was I wanted to do.[26]

This statement leaves one to wonder if perhaps the Reformed faith that Noll "eagerly and rapidly" accepted also provided him with a more secure sense of history and connectedness to the larger Christian tradition. The Reformed tradition represents itself as grounded in a historical tradition, tracing its roots to the Reformation and the orthodox theological views of the early church. Perhaps this sense of historical connectedness was missing from his former fundamentalist background.

He found his academic experience at Trinity to be quite rigorous and challenging. He listed David Wells and John Woodbridge among the professors he remembered being particularly influential. The specific contributions of these men to Noll's historical thinking will be discussed in a later chapter, but upon reflection, he did believe a great benefit he derived from his study at Trinity was to discover that the evangelical faith was one expression of a tradition that was deeply rooted in Christian history. He considers it a positive experience that some of the scholars he studied with were open to culture and dialogued with scholarship outside the evangelical world.

He finished his M. A. at Trinity in 1972 after writing a thesis on "Melchior Hofmann and the Lutherans." He then went to Vanderbilt intending to pursue Reformation studies, but the scholar he had planned to study with had left before he could begin. At this point his work became somewhat pragmatic as he needed an area of concentration in order to finish graduate school. He was interested in American Christianity and found an area of concentration in the American Revolution focusing on the relationship between Christianity and the developing nation. His dissertation examined the reciprocal relationship between religious convictions and the American Revolution.[27]

It was an interesting journey that took Mark Noll from a Conservative Baptist background in Iowa to a home in the Orthodox Presbyterian Church, from an undergraduate major in English to a Ph.D. in Church History. In many ways his journey is reflective of the one every young person must take to answer the questions of direction and purpose. It does seem though that his discovery of the Reformed faith was central to other significant decisions that occurred thereafter. Noll's comment about feeling the need to search in history to find a faith that he could "affirm whole-heartedly and which would grasp me whole-heartedly" speaks of a need for a Christian worldview that is all inclusive, one that includes the heart and mind. The Reformed tradition with its emphasis on doctrine and scholarship combined with its history of pietism seemed to provide him with this inclusive worldview. If this is true, that his Reformed faith does provide him with a Christian worldview that integrates the worlds of the mind and the heart, worlds that are often separated in evangelical life, then this raises some questions concerning his profession as a historian. How has his faith informed his view of history and perception of his role as a historian of Christianity, how does he methodologically approach the questions of history, and what pressing historical interests have occupied his time and energy? These questions will be examined in the next chapter.

Nathan Hatch

Like Mark Noll, Nathan Hatch grew up in a section of the country that could be characterized as insular. The South, insightfully observed by one Northern Presbyterian editor after the Civil War, "stacked their arms but not their principles."[28] This observation becomes more apparent to one who has grown up in the South. The term "South" is used here to refer to those states considered to be part of the antebellum south, or east of the Mississippi and south of the Mason-Dixon Line.

Nathan Hatch grew up in South Carolina during the turbulent years of the Civil Rights Movement. His family lived in Columbia, the capital of South Carolina, while his father taught Bible and Psychology at Columbia Bible College. His father was also an ordained minister of the Southern Presbyterian Church and served several churches in Mississippi before going to CBC to teach.[29] Hatch's memories were not completely clear about his family's racial attitudes or other issues of that time, but the prevailing attitudes in the South at this time, and specifically in South Carolina, were to maintain the social and religious status quo. This view amounted to social, religious, and educational segregation. A significant number of clergy in the Presbyterian Church during the 1960s took a more liberal stance on divisive social issues. The question is, how was the liberal stance on civil rights taken by some Presbyterian clergy translated in the home of a Southern Presbyterian minister teaching at a fundamentalist bible school? Was there an official position statement for the Southern Presbyterians on either issue, and if so, did this statement reflect the opinions of the Hatch household? In other words, how influential was the immediate culture in interpreting the social views shared in their home and how do these views shape a future historian?[30]

Upon reflection, Hatch admitted that it was difficult to reconstruct what his feelings and attitudes were as a child. He did remember feeling a certain distance from the Southern culture in which he was raised, and never feeling particularly patriotic about living in the South. He said he "was not a typical Southerner."[31] Since children normally acquire attitudes like patriotism and loyalty to one's region from their parents, the fact that Hatch did not feel a part of Southern culture seems to indicate that his parents did not teach or pass on to their children a self-consciously Southern heritage, and the associated cultural mores which tended to accompany that heritage. Such mores in the 1950s and 60s usually included some form of racism. Why did his parents not feel a part of Southern culture considering they had grown up in Charlotte, North Carolina?

Hatch recalled his church being predominantly white and did not remember any divisiveness in the church over the issue of race. In fact, Hatch could not recall any kind of statement being made by his church or denomination on the subject of civil rights. His father's stance on race was fairly common for white ministers in the South during the civil rights movement of the 60s. He was not in favor of segregation and was sensitive to the issues, but he was also against activism on the part of the church in protesting segregation. He was not an activist but more quietist in regard to the church's role in social and political issues.[32]

Considering that Hatch grew up in unsettled times, in a region of the country with a reputation for provincial attitudes, it is significant that he distinctly remembers feeling distant from that Southern culture. It appears that his home and its affiliation with Columbia Bible College served almost as a religious subculture in its Southern setting. The primary word Hatch used to characterize the atmosphere of CBC and his home was "open." This word was used in defining the type of fundamentalism of his environment in contrast to what he saw as a more closed and exclusive form of fundamentalism associated with other bible colleges and the prevailing religious attitudes in Southern culture. He said CBC had two themes, victorious Christian living and foreign missions. He described his father and Robert McQuilken as "open, pietistic and evangelical rather than doctrinaire." His father had been part of the Presbyterian Evangelical Fellowship in Mississippi that promoted revivalism and tended to be a more evangelistic party in the Southern Presbyterian Church.[33]

This openness translated into the manner in which his father left his sons free to choose the direction they would take in their lives. He was reticent to impose his will on his sons as his father had done to him. Hatch's father made it clear what he valued but did not impose those values on his sons. Hatch called this attitude the more gentle side of fundamentalism, an attitude which was tempered by the Keswick holiness influence of CBC. There is every indication that each son found the influence of their father and CBC appealing. The oldest son became a minister in the Presbyterian Church of America (PCA); the next son was a missionary to Latin America before dying of a sudden heart attack; Nathan Hatch pursued teaching and academics, and the youngest son became a psychologist.[34]

Nathan Hatch was always interested in politics as well as history, a subject that his father found dry and boring. He dreamed as a boy of serving as a page in Congress. Whenever his parents took trips north to the nation's capital, he would convince them to stop and allow him to visit Senator Strom Thurmond and observe a session of the Congress. His love of history motivated him in 1966, after studying two years at CBC, to transfer to Wheaton College to study history. He recalled having always wanted to leave the South to attend college and knew of Wheaton through contacts at CBC. He graduated from Wheaton *summa cum laude* in 1968 and applied to graduate school at the University of Illinois. This was the summer of 1968 when Lyndon Johnson cancelled all draft deferments due to the Tet Offensive in Viet Nam.[35] Hatch looked into Officer Candidate School but decided, upon his father's counsel, to enter Covenant Seminary in St. Louis instead.

Covenant Theological Seminary, also known as the National Seminary of the Presbyterian Church in America, is located in St. Louis, Missouri. The Evangelical Presbyterian Church founded the seminary in 1956 as an educational agency for training its ministers, but due to a denominational merger in 1982 it is now owned by the Presbyterian Church in America. Its theologically conservative tradition is founded on two primary doctrinal standards: a view of the Bible as immediately inspired by God and thus inerrant in its original writings, and subscription to the Westminster Confession of Faith and Catechisms as containing the system of doctrine consistent with the Bible. It is Reformed in doctrine and evangelical in spirit.[36]

Hatch's time at Covenant was a decisive period of his life as he struggled with the question of what to do with his future. His experience at Covenant Seminary was valuable due primarily to the students who entered with him in the Fall of 1968 and the intellectual ferment that ensued. Three very different groups of students entered that same Fall: Francis Schaeffer sent a group of Europeans from L'Abri to study at Covenant, there was an evangelical contingent that included Hatch, and a third group of Reformed students from Bob Jones University.[37] Hatch said the present faculty of Covenant who remember that Fall still talk about it to this day.

It was during his time at Covenant that Hatch considered for the first time the possibility of pursuing a secular career. While at Covenant, Hatch remembered hearing a series of lectures by Francis Schaeffer. Schaeffer's comments opened him up to the relationship between Christianity and culture.[38] Schaeffer was a proponent of the idea that the Lordship of Christ meant there was no profession intrinsically more spiritual than another. Thus to be a minister was a high calling but no more or less spiritual than a lawyer, professor, or doctor. For Christians to be called into a secular career simply meant they were to live out that calling applying a Christian worldview to what ever they chose to do.[39]

Hatch left Covenant for essentially practical reasons: the Master of Divinity degree took too long and he wanted to finish his graduate education as soon as possible. Therefore he applied and was accepted into graduate school to study history at Washington University in St. Louis. He referred to this decision as "stumbling into a superb graduate education." The two most influential professors he encountered while there were John Murrin and J. G. A. Pocock. The manner in which these men influenced Natch's historical methodology will be discussed in a later chapter, but it was here at Washington University under the direction of Murrin and Pocock that he developed the primary tools of historical inquiry and the focus of his historical interests. His dissertation involved an examination of the relationship between Republicanism and millennial thought in the early republic. After finishing his Ph.D. in History at Washington University and a Post-Doctoral Fellowship at Harvard University, he joined the History faculty at the University of Notre Dame where he presently serves as a professor and administrator.[40]

In contrast to Mark Noll, who seemed to be in search of a faith to live by and was dissatisfied with some aspects of evangelicalism as he experienced it, Nathan Hatch seemed to be more satisfied with his religious tradition but was unsure as to where to devote his life. In other words, Noll seemed to have more religious questions, while Hatch's questions were more vocational.

Subsequently, Hatch has left the Presbyterian Church to join the progressive wing of the Christian Reformed Church, which is rooted in the Dutch Reformed tradition. This tradition has historically been associated with a theology that stresses the relationship between Christianity and culture. The Christian worldview they expose affirms the Lordship of Christ over all reality. This view of lordship has most explicitly been demonstrated in the realm of education where the Reformed worldview has made significant contributions.[41] This view of reality affirms the Bible's authority and Reformed creeds as the basic tenets around which the community thrives. Rather than discovering a faith to embrace as Noll did, it seems that Hatch refined his Reformed background to match his Christian commitment to his profession. How his faith informs his work as a historian will be discussed in the next chapter.

In summary it could be said that Hatch grew up in a progressive, open, fundamentalist, home with Reformed roots. He grew up in a Southern culture but never really felt himself a Southerner. He always felt a certain distance from it. Hatch spoke of always knowing that he wanted to go away to college, sensing that there was more out there. He knew a lot about Wheaton and received a scholarship to attend as an undergraduate. He majored in history and pursued it as a profession. It would seem from the eventual faith and career decisions he made, that he found the educational and religious characteristics of his upbringing compelling enough to stay generally within that tradition.

George Marsden

Like Mark Noll, George Marsden went through a period of religious searching that challenged him to examine his faith. His search, however, was different in that he was already an heir to a fundamentalist, Reformed background; therefore, his search was one of understanding the cultural and historical roots of his own tradition rather than discovering a new one. Like Nathan Hatch, he stayed close to the roots of his childhood but, unlike Hatch, Marsden's fundamentalist home was not a progressive, open environment and thus his reasons for staying in the Reformed faith were not the same. All three men would end up relatively close to one another in terms of their faith commitments and historical interests, but for essentially different reasons.

George Marsden's was reared in a classic fundamentalist home in the sense that it echoed with the sounds of battle from the Fundamentalist/ Modernist struggles in the Presbyterian Church of the 1930s and 1940s. He remembered the cultural tension he felt when his family was ostracized by other families because they became a part of the Orthodox Presbyterians who followed J. Gresham Machen out of the Presbyterian Church in 1936. He recalled family friendships that were terminated over doctrinal and ecclesiastical decisions. Being separate and standing against the dominant culture, even against other Christians, describe his childhood recollections. How much of this did he understand? What kinds of questions would a childhood of this kind raise for a young man entering college and making life decisions?

His father counseled him to avoid Christian colleges such as Calvin College and attend the more liberal Haverford College. His father was opposed ecclesiastically to Haverford's liberal form of Protestantism, but was willing to compromise this point because of Haverford's academic standards. Therefore, at the age of 16, Marsden entered Haverford. The college had a Quaker influence and an attractive kind of humanism Marsden found enjoyable. Thus he found himself consciously interacting with two intellectual traditions, the Orthodox Presbyterian faith of his youth and a broad humanism at Haverford that was essentially incompatible with Orthodox Presbyterianism. His grandmother's liberal pietism had been his only experience of an open pietism similar to that of Haverford.[42]

Like Nathan Hatch's time at Covenant Seminary, Marsden's experience at Haverford was full of intellectual ferment. He said of this time, "I see my academic interests growing out of the questions I had of how these two worlds fit together. The things I had been brought up to believe had been dominant only one hundred years before." This colliding of two worlds was a point of tension for him. This tension was heightened by the school's pedagogical philosophy of challenging belief. He described his four years at Haverford in the following way: the first year they disabuse you of what you believe, your sophomore year you are somewhat of a skeptic, and your last two years you hopefully put all the pieces back together in a positive way. He wrote his senior thesis at Haverford on the fundamentalist controversies in the Presbyterian Church as a way of grappling with the issues he faced growing up. It does not appear his father was very helpful in this process of self-understanding. Marsden said it was extremely difficult for his father to discuss the issues of the schism without showing strong emotions. His father and others had endured a great deal of open ridicule for what they believed and this made an objective interpretation of the events of the split difficult for him.[43]

Marsden was also thinking about a future profession at this time. He considered the pastorate, but by the time of entering Haverford had given up this idea on the grounds that he was not outgoing or expansive enough for that calling. But he did find a home in academic work. The question was, which area? He considered psychology but decided against it because he found it to be too speculative. History was more attractive than psychology because he found it to be more scientific and he could get at the same questions as a macrocosm rather than as a microcosm. He decided on history and graduated with honors in 1959.[44]

However, the questions of faith that were raised during his college days were not fully answered. Therefore, after graduating from Haverford he went to Westminster Seminary. Because he had "major league" doubts about Christianity he decided he needed a better religious background. He was helped with his doubts by studying presuppositional apologetics under Cornelius Van Til. Van Til's basic premise was that one's starting point determines where one ends up intellectually; therefore, the alternatives had just as many problems as Christianity. This philosophical approach to Christianity helped to settle some of Marsden's nagging doubts about his faith.[45]

After a year at Westminster, he applied to graduate school at Yale in the field of American Studies and entered in the Fall of 1960. This proved to be a very difficult year in his life. Graduate school at Yale in the winter was depressing compared with the more collegiate atmosphere at Westminster, but the hardest part of that year was dealing with his father's unexpected death due to a heart attack. This event precipitated an intense personal crisis that lasted for a year. Marsden referred to this trying period as "going through existential angst." Life seemed meaningless, senseless, and arbitrary. He recalled sitting in a class at Yale listening to a great lecturer thinking, "if this guy is so good, why doesn't he go out and do something useful." So he quit graduate school at Yale and returned to Westminster.[46]

This time of personal crisis was finally resolved in the following summer of 1961. While serving as a counselor at a church camp in Pennsylvania he had a significant spiritual experience of personal renewal. As a result of this experience, questions about his place and purpose in God's created order were answered. After hearing and reflecting on a sermon on the twelfth chapter of First Corinthians, he understood that being part of the body of Christ made one's life and work significant. God gave each Christian gifts to be used for the good of the church. Marsden thus saw his academic abilities as intentional gifts from God to be used for God's glory and the good of the church. In speaking of this experience he said, "this experience brought my seminary training, where my intellectual questions were resolved, into congruence with my psychological and spiritual seeking of previous years." Thus with a renewed sense of religious calling and purpose, he returned to Westminster Seminary and graduated in 1963. Then, with the encouragement of Paul Wooley at Westminster, he returned to Yale to finish his studies. He finished his graduate work at Yale under Sidney Ahlstrom, writing his dissertation on New School Presbyterianism. Marsden thought it was an awful topic that no one would be interested in, which he says was true, but it did ground him in an essential understanding of the relationship between fundamentalism and Presbyterianism in the nineteenth century.[47]

Marsden's spiritual experience in the summer of 1961 appears to be crucial. It seems that this experience provided the clarity of purpose and direction he needed to finish his graduate work. In addition, it seemed to provide a framework for his understanding of why he was pursuing graduate studies in history. This initial framework become more finely tuned and nuanced in time, but it was originally conceived around the idea of seeing one's profession as a religious calling with eternal significance.

Marsden wanted to complete his theological education and then teach at Westminster as a way of fulfilling his sense of calling to serve the church through academics. But his roommate at Yale had a brother who was a professor at Calvin College and through this and other contacts Marsden accepted a position at Calvin College. Here he found a sophisticated tradition of relating Christianity to intellectual pursuits which motivated and assisted him in a deeper understanding of his calling and the relationship of that calling to his historical profession. He also found a host of other Christian scholars who were interested in examining the relationship between Christian faith and intellect which included C. T. McIntire and Nicholas Wolterstorff.[48] The Dutch Reformed tradition at Calvin provided a rich atmosphere for such discussions and Marsden quickly found a home, not only at the College but in the Dutch Reformed faith as well. He and his family are presently members of the progressive wing of the Christian Reformed Church.

Summary

When the conference on religion and politics occurred at Trinity in 1977, a convergence took place that none of those who participated had planned or foreseen. The consequent development of close friendships and academic cooperation based on common faith commitments and historical interests forms a complex and fascinating story. What began with three or four historians in 1977 has evolved over the last sixteen years into a highly visible group of accomplished and creative scholars who, as a whole, are as self-conscious about the importance of their Christian worldview as they are about the quality of their research. This dual commitment to historical scholarship and the Evangelical faith seems to be the distinctive feature that characterizes them as a group. This is not meant to suggest that all the historians who align themselves with this block of scholars are from the same faith tradition or hold the same views on the relationship between personal faith and academics, but they all engage in serious and ongoing dialogue about these issues.

George Marsden, Nathan Hatch, and Mark Noll provide the primary leadership of this unofficial but significant coterie of scholars. Because this book deals primarily with these three men there may be the impression that they speak for the rest of their colleagues in representing either a monolithic approach to historical scholarship, or a single Christian understanding of the relationship between faith and intellect or both. This impression is neither intentional nor accurate. They are not spokespersons for everyone in their particular historical school of thought; however, they do have definite distinctives that characterize the way in which they approach historical questions, and they do have a definite agenda as to the role of Christian thinking in the academic world.

A summary of the background information given in this chapter reveals some of the distinctives that characterize these three men. They, for different reasons, are all committed to the Reformed faith and to academics. Their commitment to the Reformed tradition allows them to share a common understanding of the relationship of the Christian to the world in general and academics in particular. More specifically, their commitments find expression in the Orthodox Presbyterian and Christian Reformed communities. Though the Christian Reformed Church tends to be characterized more by its views on the relationship of the Christian to culture than by doctrinal distinctives like the Orthodox Presbyterians, they both see the world and people as created by God for his pleasure and glory. It is a world that can be known and to some degree understood. Because God has created the world, then the history of the world and the people he created have eternal meaning; therefore, to study God's world and to seek understanding of it through historical research is to honor God and fulfill one's purpose as his creation. God uses all of life including the historical process to accomplish his purposes. This Reformed view perceives the Lordship of Christ as encompassing all of life, and thus the work of the professional academic is as important to God as that of the minister.

The significance of this worldview for a historian is that he or she is free to examine history for what it is, good or bad, and let the chips fall where they may. These men obviously think that Christian history is significant and they freely use the critical methods of research to examine history without fear of compromising their faith. History is a record of the past. For these men, to examine history rigorously and thoroughly and to report it carefully is to be a good historian and honoring to God. The next chapter will basically examine the historical methodology that guides their research. Specific attention will be given to their historical interests as well as their views on the relationship of faith and history.

Notes

[1] Conference Brochure, "Perspectives: The American Revolution, The American Christian, & The American Civil Religion," April 15-16, 1977.

[2] Mark A. Noll, interview by author, Tape recording, Wheaton College, Wheaton, Illinois, June 4, 1993.

[3] Ibid.

[4] Ibid.

[5] Information obtained from Personal and Curriculum Vitaes for Mark Noll, Nathan Hatch and George Marsden. Supplied to the author in November of 1992.

[6] Mark Noll Interview, June 4, 1993.

[7] Ibid.

[8] Nathan O. Hatch, interview #1 by author, Tape recording, Baylor University, Waco, Texas, December 17, 1992.

[9] George M. Marsden, *Fundamentalism and American Culture: The Shaping of Twentieth Century Evangelicalism, 1870-1925* (New York: Oxford University Press, 1980), 96.

[10] Ibid., 77-78.

[11] George M. Marsden, "Fundamentalism," in *The Encyclopedia of the American Religious Experience*, vol. 2 eds. Charles H. Lippy and Peter W. Williams (New York: Charles Scribner's Sons, 1988), 953.

[12] Nathan Hatch Interview #1, December 17, 1992.

[13] George M. Marsden, interview by author, tape recording, University of Notre Dame, Notre Dame, Indiana, June 2, 1993. For a better understanding of this mindset see Mark A. Noll and Cassandra Niemczyk "Evangelicals and the Self-consciously Reformed," in *The Variety of American Evangelicalism*, eds. Donald W. Dayton and Robert K Johnston (Knoxville: University of Tennessee Press, 1991).

[14] George Marsden Interview, June 2, 1993.

[15] Ibid.

[16] Ibid.

[17] Noll Interview, June 4, 1993. The Conservative Baptist Association of America was established in 1947. Conservative separatists founded the new denomination after giving up on their efforts at controlling the Northern Baptist Convention. This decision was reached when the Northern Baptist banned a new conservative missions organization.

[18] Marsden, *Fundamentalism*, 151-161.

[19] Noll Interview, June 4, 1993.

[20] Ibid.

[21] Mark A. Noll, interview by M. H., in *Lucas: An Evangelical History Review*, 13 (June 1992): 88-89.

[22] Mark Noll Interview, June 4, 1993.

[23] Ibid.

[24] M. H. Interview, *Lucas*, 88.

[25] Noll Interview, June 4, 1993.

[26] M. H. Interview, *Lucas*, 89.

[27] Ibid. Mark Noll, "Church Membership and the American Revolution: An Aspect of Religion and Society from the Great Awakening to the War of Independence" (Ph.D. diss., Vanderbilt University, 1975).

[28] Sydney Ahlstrom, *A Religious History of the American People*, (New York: Image Books, 1975), vol. 2, 140.

[29] Nathan Hatch, interview #1, December 17, 1992. The Southern Presbyterian Church or Presbyterian Church in the United States was formed in 1861 with the cooperation of both Old and New School Presbyterians united in their defense of the South, however, the theology of this church remained essentially Old School in character. Then, in 1983, this church united with United Presbyterian Church in the United States of America to form The Presbyterian Church (U.S.A.).

[30] Robert Wuthnow, *The Struggle for America's Soul*, (Grand Rapids: William B. Eerdmans Publishing Company, 1989), 76-77.

[31] Nathan Hatch, interview #3 by author, telephone interview, Waco, Texas, July 6, 1993.

[32] Ibid.

[33] Ibid.

[34] Hatch Interview #1, December 17, 1992. The PCA Church was formed when J. Gresham Machen left the Presbyterian Church U.S.A. and formed his own denomination.

[35] Ibid.

[36] Covenant Theological Seminary, St. Louis, Missouri, 1990-91 Catalogue.

[37] Hatch Interview #1, December 17, 1993.

[38] Ibid.

[39] Francis A. Schaeffer, *No Little People* in *The Complete Works of Francis A. Schaeffer*, (Westchester: Crossway Books, 1982), vol. 3, bk.#1, 5-14. See also Harry Blamires, *The Christian Mind*, (Ann Arbor: Servant Books, 1978).

[40] Hatch Interview #1, December 17, 1993.

[41] George M. Marsden, "Introduction: Reformed and American," in *Reformed Theology in America*, ed. David F. Wells (Grand Rapids: Baker Book House, 1989), 2-10.

[42] Marsden Interview, June 2, 1993.

[43] Ibid.

[44] Ibid.

[45] Ibid.

[46] Ibid.

[47] Ibid.

[48] Ibid.

2

Integrating Faith And Learning

This chapter is about the relationship between historical methodology and personal faith. It is an analysis of how Christian historians Mark Noll, George Marsden, and Nathan Hatch live and work in two worlds. They are committed Christians with a Reformed perspective on faith and life, and they are professional historians. They do not consciously separate their Christian beliefs from how they do historical research. They believe academics are compatible with being a Christian. But all three speak in different ways of the tensions created when trying to be true to both academics and faith.

Robert T. Handy wrote of this tension in his essay, "Christian Faith and Historical Method: Contradiction, Compromise, or Tension." Handy points out that tension exists for the Christian historian who must value empirical evidence as the core of his or her research while at the same time examining and sharing expressions of faith and personal commitment that often transcend the realm of historical methods of research.

> I suspect that there lurks a theologian and/or philosopher in most historians; the better they are aware of that and yet remain faithful to historical method, however inconvenient, the better and more acceptable historical work they will do. . . . The words "however inconvenient" suggest that there will always be tension between Christian faith and historical method, between the believer and the historian, and inside the believer who is a historian or who uses the historical method as part of the day's job. But the tension can be creative and not destructive, for within the faith itself are emphases that call some of us to do critical historical work and help all of us to see real values in the method.[1]

In order to provide a broader academic context for this discussion of methodology as it applies to the study of Christianity and history, it may be useful to digress for a moment and examine in cursory fashion the development of church history as an academic discipline. Marsden, Hatch and Noll all work in what may be referred to as the field of church history, although Mark Noll is the only one whose doctoral specialization was in church history. George Marsden's and Nathan Hatch's doctorates are in the discipline of American history. Marsden did his work in the field of American studies under Sydney Ahlstrom at Yale. Hatch also worked in the field of American studies at Washington University under John Murrin. But they all chose the History of Christianity in America as their area of interest.

They are conscious of the paradigms for doing church history that have come and gone over the past one hundred years. As stated before, these men write history while living in two camps. They are conservative, Reformed evangelicals and professional historians. Even though they do not see the need to separate these two parts of their lives, they are cognizant of the fact that their methods of doing history can and does put them in a position of being critiqued by both of these camps. Some in the evangelical camp see their method as not overtly Christian or conservative enough, thus compromising their faith, while more secular historians complain that they are too overtly Christian in their philosophy of history thus compromising their research. Therefore it will be useful to examine briefly the development of the discipline of church history in order to understand more clearly how the views of these two camps represent polarized perspectives that influence the methods and perceptions of church history. This section will also discuss how these historians address this tension.

Surveying the Discipline

Church history in America is a relatively new discipline. If one traces its official beginnings to the formation of the American Society of Church History in 1888, it is just over one-hundred years old. While many questions about the scholarly validity and value of this discipline were raised during these years, two primary questions continued to surface. The first question involved how one could discover the history of the church catholic without ending up examining all the particular churches that claim to be part of the church, and thus finish with a history of Christianity and not church history. In other words, how does one discover the true, invisible church when the only examples open to historical research are the many, varied, and often competing groups that claim to be the church? Second, can one show the providential action of God in the history of the church without violating the established canons of critical historical research?[2] In other words, one could say that Martin Luther's posting of his Ninety-Five Theses on the door of the Castle Church in Wittenberg on October 31, 1517 was a precursor to the events of the Reformation, but could one historically demonstrate the statement that in

October of 1517 God led Martin Luther to post the Ninety-Five Theses as a precursor to the Reformation?

These two approaches represent the basic tensions between faith and academics in the field of church history. Does the belief that God influences the direction of history and the choices made by people in history result in metahistory? Is the idea of the church as the invisible body of those who have experienced a spiritual transformation through redemption in Jesus Christ a historically translatable concept when speaking of the church historically? How have Christian historians sought to reconcile the tensions between faith and academics?

The last one-hundred years of church history in America have been marked by three major periods of methodological change. David Lotz, in his essay "A Changing Historiography: From Church History to Religious History," refers to the first period from 1888 to 1935 as, The Period of Church *History*, with the emphasis on history. This period was characterized by a shift in research emphasis. Previously the church was studied as a divine/human institution with the presupposition that one could research and discover the work of God in the development of the Christian church. Ephraim Emerton of Harvard and other historians felt that this paradigm for studying the church violated the use of history as an empirical science. They felt that it was better to pursue historical research from a purely inductive and objective point of view unencumbered by the theological presuppositions that influenced a previous generation of church scholars. Theology and history were therefore to be separated in the interest of pursuing a value-free history of the church. Though each could still derive benefits from the other, this separation effectively made history autonomous from theology when studying the church.[3]

The second period, 1935-1965, Lotz called, The Period of *Church* History, with the emphasis on the church. Essentially this period was a reaction to the previous period and its emphasis on inductive and objective research devoid of supernatural and theological influences. Simply put, the generation of Emerton and others appeared spiritually sterile in spite of their scholarly accomplishments. H. R. Niebuhr and others influenced by the theological movement of neo-orthodoxy saw the need to reassert the place of God in history. Theirs was a time of crisis. The world was recovering from the effects of the First World War while hovering on the brink of the Second World War. There was a need to find meaning in history, meaning that went beyond empirical evidence. The study of church history at this time was characterized by: an emphasis on history as the story of God's redemption; an ecumenical outlook that sought to find the universal church among the churches; a new relativism that employed the critical historical methods but recognized the creative role of the historian in providing an interpretation of the facts; and an autobiographical approach to church history that, in the interest of self-identity, adopted the language of faith.[4] These changes in the field of church history were paralleled by reactions in secular history against positivism.

Around 1965 this approach to church history came under scrutiny as the two questions referred to previously were again raised. Was the method of H. R. Niebuhr and others capable of discovering the hand of God in history, and was it true to the established canons of historical research? The general consensus was that the previous method had failed to demonstrate that the universal church could be discovered historically. As a result the paradigm shifted from the study of church history to the study of religious history, and the church historian became a historian of religion or of Christianity. To study the belief of a person or group of people in history was acceptable. It was not acceptable for the historian to impose his or her beliefs in providence or God on the explanation of that history.[5] Sydney Ahlstrom described this change to religious history in the following way.

> First of all, religious history has become a field of study within the larger frame of world history. It no longer enjoys any rights of sanctuary. It is allowed no immunity from the demands for evidence that historians generally make. Providence cannot be invoked as an explanatory principle. Supernatural sources of insight or knowledge cannot be claimed; though, of course, church history, like any other, benefits from learned and insightful historians who are sympathetic, deeply versed, and sensitively attuned to their subject matter.[6]

Thus it would seem that the field of church history was retaken by those historians who emphasized the need for a rigorous use of historical methods of research and disdained any attempts at theologizing the historical enterprise. But the beliefs of Emerton and others that one could approach the study of history from a value-free and objective position were rejected by many historians. This rejection would indicate that the methods of historical research were modified. The basis for this modification in historical understanding was primarily the work of several European anti-positivist philosophers of history. These men fall generally into the historicist camp which rejected many of the historical principles gleaned from the Enlightenment; such principles would include the idea that the historian is an objective observer and narrator of history. This group included Benedetto Croce, and R. G. Collingwood. It is now widely acknowledged by historians that the scholar brings his or her own beliefs, interests and prejudices to their work. In other words, the relativism of the second period of church history has continued to find strong support. The historian's work always involves interpretation, and therefore, the positivist theory that the facts alone are sufficient to tell the story lacks the credence it once enjoyed.

The issue of interpretation actually seems to be one of historical integrity. The belief that history can be written free of one's own beliefs and interests assumes that the methods of empirical science provide safe passage around one's own presuppositions. Recognizing one's on presuppositions is the beginning of objectivity. But this recognition is not a guarantee of objectivity unless history is approached from the self-conscious position of openly acknowledging one's own presuppositions and their influence on the product of their scholarship.

This brief survey of the discipline of church history has attempted to provide a larger context for a discussion of the questions of methodology in the work of George Marsden, Nathan Hatch, and Mark Noll. To reiterate, they are Christian historians. Who and what has influenced their historical methodology? Where do they fit, or do they fit, within the larger historical guild that is presently guided by this revised paradigm of historical methodology? How have they managed the tensions that seem apparent whenever personal faith and historical research interact? These are some of the questions addressed in the following section.

Historical Methods and Interests

Sydney Mead, commenting on the meaning of history, once wrote, "Each individual is the repository of all his past. History is the study of the past that has formed him. Hence the study of history is the study of one's self, and in this sense the purpose of the study is self-knowledge."[7] Mead's definition of the meaning of history as "self-knowledge" is in some ways reflective of the approach to history taken by Noll, Hatch, and Marsden. This is not exclusively so, but there are strong indicators that they approach history as an extension of who they are and not just as a professional academic exercise. This is particularly true of Noll and Marsden. Nathan Hatch seemed to be led more by his love for history than by a need to find answers to personal questions of faith. Nevertheless, all three historians have apparently found historical research to be a useful means of self-understanding.

Mark Noll

Noll's first degrees were in English rather than history. His later love for history was prompted by early interests in and wide reading of history and by personal questions about his Christian faith. These two motivations led him to seek formal historical training at Trinity College and later at Vanderbilt University. In general terms, he spoke of John Woodbridge at Trinity as being a helpful instructor in history because he stressed the importance of primary sources and gave careful attention to the explicit and implicit stages of an argument. Woodbridge was also strict in emphasizing the questions of historical proof and demonstration. Noll also mentioned Richard Wolf and Douglas Leach at Vanderbilt as helpful in that they were very close, careful readers of his work. In addition, Noll spoke of books and authors who were helpful in his historical education: E. G. Rupp and A. G. Dickens on the English Reformation, Roland Bainton's work on Martin Luther, H. E. W. Turner's work on patterns in history, and Perry Miller and Edmund Morgan for their contribution to the history of Puritanism in America. In the case of all these scholars, Noll valued the quality of their historical scholarship as well as the fact they showed some appreciation for the Christian experience in history.[8]

It would seem that during his time as a graduate student and in his early career, Noll looked for a model of scholarship that would meet the requirements of good historical research while at the same time placing value on a Christian worldview of history. As a student he primarily experienced two kinds of historical scholarship. In the evangelical world he had known the kind of history that acts more as an apologetic than as scholarship, while the historians Noll studied with at Vanderbilt showed little interests in Christian subjects. In the midst of this quandary, he began to read George Marsden's works.

> It was a revelation to see someone who quite clearly came from a conservative Protestant, theologically conservative background who was not only doing history responsibly, but who was writing witty prose and interacting in an insightful way on important themes in the history of evangelicalism. Before I ever met George he became a model for the sort of scholarship I would one day try to write. . . . It was meeting George and discovering other people in his circle that gave real stimulus to my own historical work.[9]

Marsden became the model that filled the gap for Noll between doing apologetical kinds of history and history with a primarily secular thrust. Marsden was a good historian and an openly Christian person. Particularly,

Marsden's work on Fundamentalism was crucial in its timing as it provided an example of historical scholarship that was not dismissive of a sectarian Christian tradition. In this sense it was a strategic book for Noll, Hatch, and others like Canadian historian George Rawlyk who found it extremely helpful as a model of insightful and professional scholarship done by a Christian historian.[10] It would not be overstating the case to say that George Marsden served as a kind of mentor for Noll.

Marsden influenced Noll's concept of historical methodology through his advocacy of Dutch Calvinism as a theoretical framework for doing history as a Christian. Marsden was particularly indebted to the thinking of a Dutch Calvinist named Abraham Kuyper. Abraham Kuyper (1837-1920) was a Dutch educator, Prime Minister of the Netherlands, and a theologian whose theological views launched a Neo-Calvinist movement in the Netherlands. Kuyper's concept of the Kingdom of God visualized an "organic church" that worked in the world outside of the institutional church. This church worked with an organized plan of living out Christianity in every sphere of life. In practice, this "organic church" recognized the Lordship of Christ over all areas of life. This meant two things: first, Christians needed to participate in fields such as politics, science, education and art which were previously seen by the church as worldly, and second, Christians were to bring their distinctly Christian perspective to these fields rather than participating as though they were non-Christians. This kind of Christian worldview made one's life of faith a matter of everyday life and not just a Sunday occurrence.[11] In commenting upon the consequences of this worldview for his life and work, Noll said,

> Historians can be provided with a sense of dignity for their own work which was not directly dependent on some kind of apologetical service. History, as the search for observable cause and effect that people of all sorts can talk about and debate, becomes not a substitute for faith but one way that a Christian expresses his or her faith. That's been a tremendously liberating realization in my own life and work.[12]

Dutch Calvinism also influenced Noll through its emphasis on examining presuppositions that shape people's thinking. Historians must do their work in a way that is self-conscious of their own presuppositions as well as the presuppositions of those they study. In this way Christian historians can speak to a broader audience on the reliability of historical and religious knowledge. If Christian historians do their homework and provide carefully reasoned and rigorously documented scholarship that does not seek to claim too much, then they give themselves the chance of being heard by more than just the religious world. According to Noll, "It is always best for people (historians) to show they can do the work that needs to be done methodologically self-aware and chaste in method, not trying to prove the moon."[13] Noll is very conscious of method. He accepts the general canons of historical thinking that require rigorous research and careful use of the evidence. He accepts the dictum that one cannot historically prove God raised up Martin Luther or Menno Simons. But, as a Christian historian, he believes that the study of Christianity and history can yield truth about the past, not absolute truth unaffected by the whims and fancies of human nature, but truth nonetheless. The study of history can reveal some aspects of truth because God made the world to be studied and he made the human mind in such a way that it is able to learn something true about the world. In this sense Noll is opposed to the more radical subjectivism adopted by postmodern thinkers who reject notions of discovering truth in history on the basis that historical research is so tainted by the historians personal views that the result is only fragmented knowledge, never truth.[14]

Noll believes there are advantages to examining theological and church related issues from a historical position. Christian historians have an advantage when addressing these issues within their own communities of faith because their constituency is not as apt to be looking over their shoulder as they are with Biblical scholars. The historian is not obligated to give a definitive answer to every pressing question. He or she does not have to explain everything and take a definite position. The historian is interested in providing a cohesive narrative of cause and effect that comprises the events of the past but does not have to pass final judgement on those events or the people who lived them. Consequently, more ambiguity is allowed and thus more room is given for laying out the good and bad for others to make their own judgements.

This sounds more objective than it is. The historian does have a position even if it is not an overt one, but he or she finds more latitude in telling the story by virtue of not having to make an overt judgement of right or wrong in order to present the historical narrative. Noll spoke of his work on Charles Finney and Jonathan Edwards as an example of the historian's task in presenting a cohesive narrative without the necessity of having to explain who was right or wrong. For example, Noll said that his examination of Charles Finney and Jonathan Edwards showed that the two men's views were often at odds, but, as a historian, Noll did not feel the need to defend or explain either man's position even if he believed one was more right than the other.[15]

Noll is comfortable with this historical approach to issues because he does not feel many of the biblical/theological fights among Christians have one right answer. He also feels that an approach that takes into account ambiguity and does not seek to flatten out the complexities of a problem is more reflective of the world as it is. Noll believes that this kind of approach to history is both valid and honest. He believes that a Christian should dialogue with the world. But this dialogue requires a modest realism—a realism that is not always apparent because of the dogmatic manner in which Christians often deal with one another and the world. Noll is convinced people can really know some things, especially some important things, fairly clearly. Therefore, traditional Christian answers are correct and very vital at this time in history, but need to be presented with some nuance and a demonstrated understanding of the complexities of the issues. In this way the work of the Christian historian provides the church and the world with a valuable service.[16]

One finds numerous examples of this approach in Noll's published works. He writes history self-consciously. He is aware that his subjects are chosen because he has an interest in them as a Christian and as a historian, and because he wishes to bring some aspect of history to light for the purpose of understanding. Noll is also aware, as any author is, that he is in fact writing with an audience in mind and therefore he is writing with a specific purpose. How he writes and what he writes is affected by who he writes for. He writes for the church and the world. He writes for those who have Christian interests and are part of a Christian community, and he writes for a more secular audience as a historian specializing in the contribution of Christianity to American history.[17]

In both instances he adheres to the accepted standards of historical research. His method is chaste and rigorous, acknowledging the necessity of using appropriate empirical data. His interpretations do not rely upon appeals to divine providence but neither do they debunk the Christian church's testimony to the work of God. Noll takes the historical data seriously without assuming an anti-supernatural stance toward religious issues. When a historian does not take an anti-supernatural stance in regard to religious subjects it has often been assumed that the end product is a triumphal Christian history that overlooks the fallible, human side of Christianity. Noll seems to avoid this problem of triumphalism by using history to critique his own evangelical tradition and Christian history as a whole. Rather than taking a party line toward the past, Noll raises questions about the attitudes and actions of Christians, specifically evangelical

Christians, in American history. Secular historians, who value historical objectivity, welcome this approach to religion. Some in the Christian community, however, find this approach unacceptable because it questions and critiques many of the perceptions that shape the thinking of their community.

Noll's book, *A History of Christianity in the United States and Canada*, is an illustration of his approach to writing history as a Christian historian. The self-conscious nature of his approach is immediately recognizable in the introduction to the book. In the introduction, Noll does far more than give a synopsis of the book's contents. He openly acknowledges that information is never presented objectively because presuppositions shape the selection and presentation of the material. In effect, a history book argues a thesis that is either implicit or explicit. Noll seeks to make his argument and approach as explicit as possible.[18]

He acknowledges the influence of recent scholarship and its emphasis on recording the experiences of the common people as opposed to writing history exclusively from above or from the perspective of the affluent and powerful in society. Thus he conspicuously includes groups that tend to be marginalized in histories adopting a Protestant British narrative model such as Winthrop Hudson's *Religion in America*. The experience of slavery and the rise of the black churches are included along with the role of women, native Americans, Hispanics, Mormons, Millerites, and other alternative religious communities. But he also states that his work "swims against the tide of recent scholarship" in that Noll is not writing a history of religion in America but rather a history of Christianity, and thus his research focuses more on Christianity than on America. The basic question he raises is, what distinctive features have characterized Christianity's development in the American social context? He is concerned primarily with Christian sources that have disclosed the interpretations and experiences of those who called themselves Christians, and he acknowledges this dependence by stating, "My readings may all be wrong, but at least it should be clear where they are coming from: they are coming from the perspective of a Christian who happens to live in the United States."[19]

Noll's criteria for determining who the Christians were in American society consists of two questions. Did a group see itself as Christian, and did others recognize them as being Christian? He qualifies this standard by stating that sympathy with those who called themselves Christians is "not to endorse every belief, institution, practice, or opinion reported." He further states that as a historian he reserves the right to exercise charity in regard to who could be called a "true Christian." Noll concludes his introduction by quoting from the French scholar Claude-Jean Bertrand who accused American churches of contributing to puritanism, philistinism, manicheanism, and racism while at the same time lauding them for nourishing dynamism, egalitarianism, tolerance, generosity, humanity and idealism. Noll comments that the contradictions found in Bertrand's appraisal provide fertile ground for inquiring into the whys and wherefores of such observations of American Christianity.

Noll's introduction is extremely self-conscious and intentional in its desire to avoid any misunderstandings about the perspective from which he writes the book. This does not make the introduction an apology for the material selected or for the perspective of the author, but rather it demonstrates Noll's deliberate approach to history: one that is conscious of alternative philosophies of history and of the interests and presuppositions that drive historians.

Noll is also careful to show that his history of Christianity in America will not be another triumphal narrative. Noll's historical approach, as informed by his Christian faith, reveals a healthy degree of skepticism where the intentions and actions of people are concerned. Just because people claimed they were Christians, the world still had the right to examine their lives and actions to judge whether their claim were true. To examine the history of those who called themselves Christians is to examine not only their attitudes and actions but also the consequences of those attitudes and actions as they affected others in that society. In this vein Noll stated, "I expect to find in efforts to reconstruct the past both great human accomplishments and great human failure, comedy and tragedy, and nowhere more directly than in the story of the Christian Church."[20]

In *Between Faith and Criticism*, Noll wrote a historical essay addressing how evangelicals approached the issue of Biblical scholarship as it developed over the last one-hundred years. He identified his audience as those who considered themselves evangelicals and those who did not. This could have included those who did not consider themselves Christians as well. Rather than defining evangelicals theologically, for historical purposes, Noll defined them in terms of "interlocking institutions, personal networks, and common traditions." He referred to this approach as descriptive rather than prescriptive. In this work he attempted to relate how evangelicals think about the authority of the Bible and how this influenced the ways in which they dealt with higher-critical Biblical scholarship. He also tried to assist in an understanding of the tensions that were created when evangelical scholars found themselves debating Biblical issues in an increasingly skeptical and secular age that gradually marginalized orthodox Christian views. This increasing secularization isolated some evangelical scholars and created a bifurcated approach to biblical issues within the Christian community. Evangelical scholars wanted to be recognized by the academic world while not loosing the blessing of their church. The desire to achieve academic respectability while remaining true to traditional religious beliefs created an ironic scenario for future generations of evangelicals.

> As the sons, and later daughters, of a minority subcommunity go to universities, and eventually to the best universities, the community swells with pride. But when a few of the scholars return to repudiate the community values or to propose even their modest restructuring, confusion, antagonism, and consternation result.[21].

Noll declared his own convictions that evangelical views on the Scriptures were valid and should be presented in the free market place of ideas. But he cautioned that if evangelicals were to reenter the world of academic discussion they must first develop a theology of criticism. This theology of criticism should be a more self-conscious approach to theological research, one which allowed evangelicals to take their discussion beyond their own communities and engage a wider field of biblical scholarship.

Once again Noll exhibited a style that was very deliberate in defining purpose, audience, and issues. Biblical issues can be extremely volatile among evangelicals because of the serious manner in which they approach the Scriptures. Noll believes being a historian is an advantage when dealing with potentially divisive biblical and theological issues. The historian's advantage is that he or she does not have to take a final position on an issue in order to provide a cohesive historical narrative.

Noll's research on the relationship between evangelicals and biblical scholarship provided him the opportunity to address a reoccurring point of conflict among evangelicals from a historical perspective. Often a different perspective offers an alternative means for dealing with difficult issues. Noll was hopeful that a historical approach would provide a platform for further discussion and, perhaps, some resolution of this issue. One is left to wonder if Noll was among those sons who went off to the university and came home to repudiate his community's values or to suggest a restructuring of them only to be met with scorn. Instead of giving up on the community, however, he chose to address the issues from an angle that could be useful to the community. The next chapter explores how Noll's method of writing history, his historical interests, and his questioning of some Christian interpretations of American history, caused him to cross theological and cultural boundaries thus making his scholarship suspect in the eyes of some evangelicals.

Nathan Hatch

Nathan Hatch liked history and politics as a youth. His interest in these two subjects did not diminish over the years but were nurtured and developed through high school and later as a history major at Wheaton College. In the Fall of 1970 he entered Washington University, located in St. Louis, Missouri, as a graduate student in American History. He referred to this period in his life as "stumbling into as superb graduate education." It was at Washington University that two professors left an indelible imprint upon his thinking as a student of history.[22]

Hatch found Professor John Murrin to be one of the smartest and most incisive men he had ever met. He was impressed by Murrin's grasp and knowledge of the historical sources and by his keen and creative mind. Hatch remembered the dialogue from his seminars with Murrin in which Murrin in the course of the discussion "would throw out a dissertation idea a minute." Hatch said Murrin was "always turning theories in his head." From Murrin, Hatch learned that a good historian always analyzes the ruling assumptions of a given historiography. The contribution of a historian was to examine the ruling assumptions to determine if in fact the evidence fit the assumption. If not, if another unseen angle better explained the evidence, an angle that would alter the previous assumptions, then the historian was in a position to make a contribution to his field. In other words the historian needs to ask if another interpretive model makes better sense of the facts.

Murrin's contribution to this process of examining a given historical model was his refutation of the idea that the American colonists in 1776 ceased to be Englishmen and that the consequential feelings of estrangement from England precipitated the American Revolution. Murrin proposed that the opposite was true; that in fact the colonists were more like Englishmen in 1776 than they ever would be again, and the Revolution was a struggle by the colonists to have a society like England and be free Englishmen. He called this his theory of Anglicanization.[23]

The fact that this principle of challenging assumptions became a crucial part of Hatch's own historical methodology is apparent from a reading of his Yale University Bartlett Lecture, "The Puzzle of American

Methodism," delivered on February 9, 1993. In this lecture, Hatch pointed out that the last thirty years witnessed sweeping changes in the approach scholars took to religion in America. Furthermore, in this lecture, Hatch's basic question was, with all the positive changes that have taken place in the study of religion in America over the last thirty years, why have scholars virtually ignored the role of Methodism in the development of early American society? Hatch contended that no scholar championed the cause of American Methodism as Perry Miller did for the Puritans. He reasoned that this oversight resulted from the perception that most scholars had of early Methodism.

> I am convinced that American Methodism is a historical gold mine that awaits serious quarrying. Quite simply, Methodism remains the most powerful religious movement in American history and it appeared at the most crucial juncture in our history. The fault is not in the sources, nor in the number of indicators pointing to their importance. The fault lies within our own historical conventions, the basic framework, the set of assumptions which have governed the way scholars have approached American religious history. ["Patterns sanctified by great historiographic traditions become fixed," J. H. Hexter noted. "Frequently these patterns are neither logical nor coherent, but the sanctions of use behind them is so powerful that researchers tend to force new materials into the time-honored models."][24]

Hatch believed the fault for ignoring the contribution of Methodism to American history lay in the invalid assumptions of scholars who drew their assumptions from equally invalid historiographical traditions. On the basis of this belief Hatch set out to examine three points. Why did Methodism virtually explode between the Revolution and the Civil War to become the most populous denomination? Considering this early success, why have scholars been inoculated from interest in Methodism, and why is Methodism a better prototype than Puritanism for explaining the dynamics of American religious life?

Hatch contended that part of the neglect of Methodism was located in the strong influence of Puritan studies on religious history. These studies emphasized the flow and development of Puritan intellectual traditions founded upon Puritan theology. Thus the American religious experience had been primarily construed in terms of intellectual history. Methodism's belief in revivalism, its anti-intellectual thrust, popular romanticism, and emotionalism did not easily fit the mold of intellectual history. This failure to meet the prevailing historical standards for intellectual history made

Methodism less than attractive to many scholars, but it also had a second more serious effect.[25]

Those scholars with Methodist backgrounds who did attempt to write histories of their tradition tended to sanitize their histories to make Methodism more presentable. They often presented Methodism as the bearer of civilization to the backward and uncouth frontier while de-emphasizing the bold, passionate, and unrefined style of frontier revivalism which contributed significantly to the growth and popularity of Methodism. In other words these types of histories attempted to make Methodism respectable to a modern religious community that valued intellectual depth, liturgical order, and an ecumenical spirit.[26]

In addition to John Murrin, Hatch also benefited from his association with J. G. A. Pocock. Pocock specialized in the political thought of the early American period. His major contribution to Hatch's thinking was in his constantly asking the question, what was it possible for a given generation of people to think? One must study the past as if the future never happened. The people of any given time period made decisions and lived out their lives without knowing what it was all leading to, and therefore, they should be studied with this perspective in mind. The pastness of the past cannot be overcome, and, therefore, many assumptions about the past often prove to be fallacious. Thus the ironies of history are important evidence of people being often unaware of the consequences of their actions. Pocock therefore disliked the Whig interpretation of history which examined all history with an underlying presupposition of progress. This view led Whig historians to handle the events of history as a simple matter of observable cause and effect. This type of historical interpretation left no room for irony and assumed on the past an understanding largely informed by the historians own present.[27]

In his book, *The Democratization of American Christianity*, Hatch heeded Pocock's admonition about writing history. Hatch took the position that the shape of Christianity in America was as much the product of unintentional actions and decisions as it was the product of carefully planned and executed agendas. He wrote, "The rise of democratic Christianity in the early United States is riddled with irony, unrealistic hope, and unfulfilled expectations. A central theme of the chapters that follow is the unintended results of people's actions."[28] Hatch provided an example of this phenomenon when describing the strife that occurred when the lay population in the early American republic sought to close the gap between themselves and the clergy by breaking away from more formal religion to choose their own clerics. This decision proved to be a double-edged sword because in gaining new freedom over the choice of their own pastors they unknowingly set up a system which allowed for the rise of religious demagogues. The freedom that denominational fragmentation brought in the new republic was matched by the autonomous power of new religious leaders.[29] Hatch further warned against a Whig interpretation of history when he delivered the O. C. and Grace Tanner Lecture in May of 1993. Speaking before a large audience of Mormon historians he chose the topic, "Mormon and Methodist: Popular Religion in the Crucible of the Free Market." Mormon history, like Methodist history, was usually written as denominational history. In other words it had the strength of being passionate and exact, but it also exhibited the weakness of limited interpretation.

> The besetting sin of believers as historians is the fallacy of Whig history, to survey the historical landscape with a preference for that which is similar to, or that which anticipates, the present. Thus the ecumenist, when coming to history, finds its direction and movement in ecumenical successes, the high-church devotee in the church's organic development, the pacifist in peace movements, and the fundamentalist in militant defense of the truth, the social activist in examples of reform. Once we begin with our own commitments, the selection of the facts to fit them is all to easy, the more so since selectivity is usually unconscious. The parts of the story which we underline are very often merely just the ones that seem important because they bear out our own convictions.[30]

Hatch went on to demonstrate this problem of Whig history by utilizing his reading of Mormon history. He said that Mormon history was normally connected with the person of Joseph Smith, a man considered to be a divine prophet who led a fiery sectarian movement that burst the bonds of the religious and social status quo. But today's Mormon history was more likely to focus on Mormons as patriotic and hard-working people who emulated middle class values and the Protestant work ethic. "Mormonism today seems more attuned to the upscale image of Marriot hotels and to the melodious strains of the Mormon Tabernacle Choir" rather that reflecting "what Edith Wharton referred to as 'the underside of the social tapestry where the threads are knotted and the loose ends hang'."[31] Mormons have, like the Methodists, sanitized their history to make it more representative and acceptable to the present age.

Hatch adopted these two basic tenets of historical interpretation learned from Murrin and Pocock and applied them in his own areas of interest, history and politics. In addition to his most recent book, *The Democratization of American Christianity*, his dissertation was an attempt to combine the work of Pocock and Bernard Bailyn, another influential historian, to demonstrate a connection between Republican ideology and millennial thinking in Revolutionary America. Yale University Press later published his dissertation under the title, *The Sacred Cause of Liberty: Republican Thought and the Millennium in Revolutionary New England.*[32] Bernard Bailyn's prescription for good history influenced Hatch. Bailyn, in an essay entitled, *History and the Creative Imagination*, listed those historians he considered critical and significant for historical understanding. The essential criteria that qualified one for this auspicious group was scholarship that transformed the subject of history by shifting it to a new plane of understanding. This, for Bailyn, was the mark of a creative historian. Such a historian was characterized by four traits. First and foremost, the historian must be able to ask good, new questions of the data. He accomplishes this task by using his imagination to conceive of a new reality beneath the reality. The creative historian can look beneath the surface of the facts and see a vague, undiscovered new world that has eluded others. Next the historian must contextualize that new world by challenging the interpretations of other historians whose work obscured the real past. He then forms and develops his alternative interpretation through the use of new or previously undiscovered data, and finally, through the use of key figures and events, he weaves together the threads of essential relationships to complete the tapestry of this new world.[33]

Hatch was taught that the facts of history were like iron filings. Without the creative mind of the historian they were formless. But through the process of asking good questions, carefully studying the available evidence, and finding new cashes of data, the facts of history could be creatively shaped and formed into an interpretation that provided a window through which the events of the past took on meaning. The difference between a good historian and an average one was this creative instinct. Hatch referred to this process of doing history as "studying ideas as hammered out in practice, trying to understand the worldview of an era. This is a common sense approach, not laden with great methodological apparatus."[34] But at the same time he was keen on the idea that amidst the rigorous research there needed to be a fertile and imaginative mind capable of bringing creativity to the historical process.

On the question of how religious faith informs and shapes historical positions, Hatch readily admitted that his Christian faith did inform his historical perspective, but in the same way that anyone's worldview influences their thinking. He rejected the idea of personal objectivity in historical research. It is not objectivity that is crucial, but rather it is having a conscious awareness of one's own prejudices and then having the honesty to admit them openly. Hatch believes people are not truly objective, and therefore need to admit their prejudices. He felt the worst thing to do was to say that you were objective and then have these unspoken prejudices swirling under the surface.

Hatch's historical perspective was influenced by his Christian worldview, but also by his reading of progressive historians like Carl Becker and Charles Beard. Both of these American historians of the early twentieth century rejected the idea of history as an objective, "value-free" science. They believed that there were hidden, or a least unspoken, purposes and agendas behind the desire to be objective. Becker once wrote, "Even the will to be objective is itself a purpose, becoming not infrequently a passion, creating the facts in its own image."[35] Becker also believed that the past, except for our ideas of it, was irretrievable. Therefore the ideas and events of the past could not speak for themselves. The past was to be understood in relationship to the experiences and understanding of the present,[36] however, the tendency of historians was to superimpose upon the past an interpretive framework shaped by the ideas and beliefs of the present without carefully differentiating between the framework and the actual history.

In this regard Hatch advocates a broad framework for understanding and writing history. He writes principally about religion but believes that it is best to understand religion and Christianity from the context of the broader culture, taking into account political, and social history as well as religious history. This approach allows for a broader range of historical questions and thus avoids the pitfall of "studying the influence of religion upon religion upon religion." Hatch thinks that the best church histories and religious histories were grounded in their own time. He referred to two ways of becoming a historian of Christianity in America. One could approach religious studies as a historian of America who studies Christianity, or one could study church history. Hatch believed the first option was better. He supported this view by observing that the most creative religious historians of his generation came out of history departments. He contended this was due to the broader perspective they had for approaching the questions of history.[37]

In addition to pursuing history from a broad perspective, Hatch thought that people who pursued academic life out a sense of religious calling, (a strong inclination that there is divine providence involved in one's vocation), exhibited something dynamic in their work. He related this dynamic quality to the foundation these people had in their religious tradition, a foundation that lent intensity to their quest for knowledge. He observed this characteristic in the young Mormon historians he addressed in the Tanner Lecture. Hatch called it a kind of passion that drives their historical search. He said this intensity affected the quality of work produced by a previous generation. For example, church historians like Martin Marty, Robert Handy, Sydney Ahlstrom, and William Hutchison came from a mainline sense of faith seeking understanding and turned out a vast array of fine historical work. In reflecting upon the recent success of young evangelical historians, Hatch believed that their success was due in part to the sense of religious calling they felt in their historical work. This sense of calling came from their foundation in a religious tradition that generated a passion for their subject and drove them to excel. He further stated that he was saddened by the seeming loss of interest in religious history among the present generation of historians coming out of mainline traditions. He attributed this lack of interest to a loss of passion for their own traditions, a symptom of their general turning away from religious subjects to more secular interests. In comparison, he saw the work of evangelical historians as reflective of a desire to interface religious distinctives with scholarly excellence. Hatch was convinced that this combination produced a creative energy that characterized their work.[38]

A number of people and ideas shaped Nathan Hatch's historical understanding and methodology. From John Murrin he learned to question the prevailing historical paradigms in order to determine whether the accepted interpretations of the day best fit the evidence. J. G. A. Pocock taught him always to ask what it was possible for the people of a certain time and place to believe, thereby avoiding the mistake of imposing the views of the present on the past. He learned to value the irony of history. Things do not always turn out as they were planned. Bernard Bailyn taught him that creativity and imagination in shaping and evaluating historical evidence were the signs of a good historian. Asking the right questions and finding new data were essential prerequisites to a better understanding of the past. Like Beard and Becker, Hatch rejected the idea of history as a "value-free" science. While one had prejudices, awareness of these prejudices assisted a historian in differentiating between his or her personal beliefs and those of a past generation. Hatch's own experience led him to believe that a sense of religious calling is an asset for a historian of religion, but one which also needs to be grounded in the broadest possible context for providing a better understanding of religious history. Passion and intensity have a place in scholarship. Having a sense of foundation in a religious tradition and working from that distinctive position provides significant energy and motivation for Nathan Hatch's historical research.

George Marsden

George Marsden's approach to American religious history is consistent with Nathan Hatch's description of a historian who comes at his or her subject as a historian of American history who studies religion. Marsden received his formal historical training at Haverford College under medieval historian Wells McCaffery and later at Yale under Sydney Ahlstrom and Edmund Morgan. While at Haverford he developed a love for history but struggled in deciding whether to pursue graduate studies in history or psychology. Marsden was intrigued with the study of human behavior and theories of personality, but his personal questions about religion and family provided the subjects for his historical research.

Marsden's senior thesis at Haverford on the Fundamentalist controversies in the Presbyterian Church provided him a way of grappling with his own personal experiences growing up. He also speculated as to the better avenue for studying religious and cultural questions, history or psychology. Eventually he decided against psychology because he found it to be too speculative. He felt that all the grand theories and paradigms for looking at human nature were essentially the same, and he determined that the study of history allowed for a more scientific approach to questions of culture and religion.[39]

His educational experiences at Haverford, Yale, and Westminster were formative both academically and religiously. At Yale he pursued a masters degree and a doctorate in American Studies. He wrote his dissertation on New School Presbyterianism. Between completing his masters degree (1961) and doctorate (1965) at Yale, Marsden finished a B. D. (1963) at Westminster Theological Seminary. This period at Westminster was a time of intellectual and spiritual turmoil for Marsden as he struggled with "major league" doubts about his faith. In his first year at Westminster he was helped in his struggles by Cornelius Van Til. Van Til's course in presuppositional apologetics provided Marsden with a method for critiquing the ideas of modern culture, specifically the Enlightenment idea of a "value-free" science. In reflecting back on his time with Van Til, Marsden believes Van Til's critique of the Enlightenment and its influence on Christianity was close to that of present day postmodernist. Van Til, like the postmodernists, believed the idea of a "value-free" science was an illusion.

After his first year at Westminster, Marsden was accepted at Yale for graduate work, but despondency over his father's death in 1960 caused him to leave Yale and return to Westminster. In the summer of 1961, Marsden attended a church camp where he experienced a renewal of his faith that led him to commit himself to the pursuit of academic studies for the glory of God. He described his commitment in this way, "my religious experience brought me back into a sense of religious calling, using my gifts for the benefit of the church, to use my intellectual powers to serve the church through scholarship. . . . This sense of calling brought my seminary training, where my intellectual questions were resolved, into congruence with my psychological and spiritual seeking of the previous year."[40] Marsden's realization that his personal faith was a calling that united his commitment to God with his intellectual pursuits was a pivotal point in his life. He returned to seminary with enthusiasm and a sense of purpose that motivated him to finish his B. D. in theology. He then returned to Yale where, in 1965, he completed his doctorate in American Studies under Sydney Ahlstrom.[41]

Marsden's education was a time of searching and questioning as he sought to integrate his Christian faith with his intellectual pursuits. The intellectual challenges of Haverford caused him to question the validity of his Christian beliefs. He valued education and even decided to pursue academics as a vocation, but he was torn by the intellectual and spiritual questions that academics raised for his faith.

One can assume that his training in history at Haverford and Yale taught him to employ rigorously the accepted methods of the discipline. He stated that he chose history over psychology because he appreciated the scientific approach historians took to questions of culture and human behavior. He studied at Yale under Sydney Ahlstrom and Edmund Morgan, two leading historians of American religious history with impeccable credentials.

Like Hatch and Noll, Marsden was a student of history, but he was also driven by a Reformed perspective. The question for Marsden was not really one of method as much as one of how to integrate method with faith. How does a evangelical historian write history that is shaped by the established canons of historical research? He could just write history, but it was important for him to understand the theoretical and metaphysical issues of writing history as an evangelical Christian.[42]

In 1965 he joined the faculty of Calvin College, a small liberal arts college with a Dutch Reformed tradition. There he found a sophisticated tradition of relating Christianity and the intellect, and he became involved in an ongoing discussion among members of the faculty over the issue of how faith and intellect interact. In 1975 he co-edited a book that grew out of these discussions. *A Christian View of History* represented views of history essentially consistent with a those of the Reformed thinker Abraham Kuyper. Marsden outlined his perspective on a Christian approach to writing and teaching history in his essay "A Christian Perspective for Teaching History."

Marsden believes that the perspective or worldview from which one approaches the study of history is critical. Marsden does not believe it is possible to study history or any other subject from a completely objective point of view. It is necessary to be aware of and admit to one's own prejudices and cultural biases. The product of this personal baggage check is not always good history, but hopefully, if one lays the cards on the table, a more open dialogue will result. Marsden, like Sydney Mead, thinks the final purpose of historical study is self-understanding and the understanding of others. Marsden believes if Christians are to love people they must seek to understand them, and historical research can help provide an essential understanding of others.[43]

History as memory is another important aspect of understanding. A person or society has a past partially comprised of those experiences stored away as memories. These memories, in turn, are an important part of that person's or society's history. If that history is to be helpful in self-understanding it must be meaningful. Thus the historian must apply interpretation to history if he or she is to help in providing a meaningful past. This is the point at which worldview is crucial because the historian employs, consciously or unconsciously, a value system which affects this process of selecting and interpreting the facts of history. How does a Christian historian go about the task of selecting and interpreting facts, and is it different from a non-Christian historian's approach?

Marsden points out that from the outset the Christian historian will differ in terms of his or her view of reality and anthropology. He assumes, from his perspective as an evangelical, that the Christian will perceive reality in terms of a created order. God has created the world as we know and experience it, and thus there is a divine anthropology. We are God's creation, and, as such, it follows that people have a moral responsibility as the highest part of God's creation. Marsden believes that this sense of moral responsibility will affect the Christian historian's view of history.[44] It is important to understand Marsden's view that the events of history take place in a created world. A created world necessitates a creator. He rejects a naturalistic interpretation of reality in which events occur by chance in a closed system.

Marsden believes that the facts are the same for both Christian and non-Christian but that their interests and purpose for studying history will differ. When the Christian historian chooses facts that provide the best understanding of his or her tradition, this does not mean that history is distorted any more than when a Marxist selects facts that best illustrate that position—provided the interpretation is balanced showing both gold and dross. Sir Herbert Butterfield in his book *Christianity and History* argues this same point.

> Therefore, the liberal, the Jesuit, the Fascist, the Communist, and all the rest may sail away with their militant versions of history, howling at one another across the interstellar spaces, all claiming that theirs is the absolute version, admitting no place even for an academic history that shall be a bridge between them. . . . But while we have Marxists, and Wellsians, Protestants, and Catholics with their mutually exclusive systems, many people, confounded by the contradictions, will run thankfully in the last resort to the humbler academic historian—to the man who will just try to show what can be established by the concrete external evidence, and will respect the intricacy and the complexity of events, bringing out the things which must be valid whether one is a Jesuit or a Marxist.[45]

Marsden argues for an interpretation that is both explicit and implicit; explicit in the openness of stating one's purpose, implicit in acknowledging that answers are not always clear and thus what is known can be true without being known perfectly. He then gives a kind of Christian epistemology by discussing four areas that reflect an evangelical Christian's knowledge of the world.

Marsden begins with the idea that the Christian God acts in human history. The belief that he has acted and continues to act is derived from the record of his character and actions found in the Christian Scriptures. As a result of these scriptures the Christian knows that history is important because the climax of history will be a judgement on the actions of humanity. Biblical records do more than tell what happened. They often provide the explanation of why it happened, a luxury not usually found in secular historical records. The Christian can see history as providential but providing interpretation for historical events is tenuous at best.[46] There is a note of caution here for the Christian historian who wants to read the hand of God into every historical event. History can be providential without being clear. A historian cannot afford to act like a tugboat captain who blows his horn the loudest when the fog is thickest.

A second area of knowledge involves the Biblical view of people. Marsden believes that the Bible describes people as a paradox. They are simultaneously the height of God's creation and rebels estranged from God. Even those who have been reconciled to God are defined by Martin Luther as, *simul justi et peccator*, simultaneously a sinner and yet justified or forgiven. Marsden wrote, "The Christian historian, with such knowledge that man is capable of being both the crown and the scum of the universe, views man's cultural achievements in this perspective. He therefore recognizes both the genuine values of the accomplishments of the race, but also points out how these same accomplishments form the bases for man's self-centered view of the world, and for his self-deceptive false religions."[47] Marsden sees this view exemplified in an evangelical Christian's interpretation of the Enlightenment. The Enlightenment of the seventeenth and eighteenth-centuries showed people were capable of great achievements and great arrogance. Intellectual advancements and scientific freedoms were achieved along with the recognition of unjust social conditions. But along with this advancement came the belief that reason could discover comprehensive natural laws governing the universe and the moral laws needed to eliminate injustice and other social ills. For the Enlightenment thinkers, these reasonable moral laws made a belief in transcendental laws based on divine revelation unnecessary. Marsden does not imply that Christian historians should set up an artificial good guy bad guy scenario, but rather, he believes they should recognize that the best attempts of people to create a moral system void of God is fraught with error. "Our purpose in studying history is not primarily to condemn others who have made mistakes, but rather to understand ourselves in relation to others and to culture."[48]

Marsden stresses the need to analyze cultural values carefully as a way of discovering the implicit forces that drive society. This stress on cultural values has marked Marsden's work as a historian of American Christianity. Almost every area of his work is shaped by the idea that we are, consciously or unconsciously, indebted to the culture in which we are raised for our ideals and values, and that these ideals and values influence the choices we make and the manner in which we perceive life. "My analysis of cultural influences on religious belief is a study of things visible. As such, it must reflect sympathy with the modern mode of explanation in terms of natural historical causes. Yet it would be a mistake to assume that this is incompatible with a view of history in which God is the dominant force, and in which other unseen spiritual forces are contending."[49] Marsden's scholarship on the many facets of

Fundamentalism is particularly reflective of this principle. Marsden believes historians should consider the personal and professional cultural forces that have shaped them and their interests.

> In this important task of exposing untested assumptions that shape us and our culture, the role of the historian is analogous to that of the psychoanalyst. In somewhat the same way that unconscious and subconscious factors influence our psychological development, deep-seated cultural patterns, ideals, values, and assumptions exert a subtle and often unrecognized influence on everyone in that culture. To the extent that these influences remain unconscious we are controlled by them; but to the extent that we are made conscious of these influences we are in a position to discriminate among them and to exercise a degree of control over them. . . . The historian brings cultural patterns, ideals, values, and assumptions to consciousness by tracing them back to their historical origins. If only the present is considered, current political and social patterns, as well as general cultural ideals, often appear to have a certain inevitability about them.[50]

Marsden states that one of the roles of the historian is to test the prevailing social and religious assumptions by examining the historical roots of those assumptions. The value of this testing process is found in the uncovering of mere slogans and or myths that have posed as truth. "The Christian historian, like the non-Christian, does valuable service if he does no more than to clear the minds of his audience of some of the nonsense of the slogans and mythologies of his era."[51] What Marsden does not say is that some of the historian's audience may not appreciate his or her efforts in clearing up "some of the nonsense." Some of the audience may have strong attachments to the slogans and myths.

Marsden identifies human motivation as another important area of the Christian historian's knowledge. Why do people act the way they do? What motivates someone to choose one thing over another? Marsden takes into account the supernatural as a factor in human choices. He accepts the role of the Holy Spirit in changing people's lives and in influencing their decisions. However, the difficulty is determining the primary factor for those choices and relating these factors to historical knowledge. There could be explanations other than the Holy Spirit such as culture, background, immediate pressures, or health, to name a few. Marsden's view of the Bible, as stated before, is a cautious one that acknowledges incongruity and complexity. The Bible gives examples of people making choices for a variety of reasons ranging from a love for God to greed, jealousy, and power. Marsden contends that the Christian historian, while not ruling out the supernatural, takes into account the complexity of people and the forces that influence them for both good and ill.[52] An equally difficult problem is that of being able to verify the sources of influence on people's lives. Even though a Christian historian may acknowledge the existence of the supernatural, there is still the problem of historically verifying the supernatural as a source of influence.

Finally, Marsden contends that the Christian historian's interpretation will be shaped by moral and value judgements. He concedes that while moral and value judgements will occur, the question is, how overt should these judgements be. Marsden appeals for a sympathetic approach with a dash of humor. In contrast to an approach that sees a moral lesson in every historical event or one that excludes moral judgements entirely, Marsden believes that other people's mistakes are usually our own as well. One can analyze the events of history and discuss them in terms of moral implications without wholesale condemnation. This analysis is best done with a sense of humor and a dose of humility.[53] What is condemned in others is often lost on our own sensibilities. If self-understanding is the point of historical study then one must consider seriously the continuity we have with the successes and failures of past humanity.

George Marsden's approach to history mixes historical methods with a keen awareness of one's own worldview. He acknowledges an indebtedness to the canons of modern historical studies but does not believe those canons require him, as a professor and scholar, to preclude his Christian faith. He rejects, with Hatch and Noll, the idea of history as a "value-free" science. Historians, like other professionals, are encumbered by cultural baggage that affects their perspective and interests. Marsden's own interests have focused on the cultural background and intellectual traditions that have shaped nineteenth and twentieth-century American Fundamentalism. He admits that this interest grows out of his own background and the questions that were raised during his years growing up in a fundamentalist home.

Marsden is interested in the theoretical issues of writing history, particularly questions related to how an evangelical Christian historian integrates faith and learning. Marsden is a disciple of Abraham Kuyper in that he rejects the idea of a spiritual/secular dichotomy. He believes, with Kuyper, that the Christian's life forms a unity of mind, body, and spirit, and therefore, a Christian should apply his or her faith in all areas of life. Consequently, Marsden's interpretation of history includes a providential dimension. Like historians with more secular interests, he examines the evidence using the methods of historical research. Unlike some other historians, Marsden sees history occurring in a world created by a personal God who participates in that history.

Marsden brings a Biblical view of people to his research. People are valuable, made in the image of God, but they are also stinkers, capable of great evil. While he accepts the supernatural as a valid source of explanation for the actions and motivations of people, he is reticent to make the supernatural the primary or only explanation. Marsden believes that there are other factors that must be accounted for, such as culture and personality.

Because he believes people are made in the image of a personal God, Marsden takes seriously the idea of moral responsibility. People make choices that matter. Those choices and the motivations behind them are the stuff of history. This does not, however, place the historian in the position of playing God. The historian should exercise restraint in condemning or praising the actions of the past. Caution, grace and a sense of humor are the best characteristics for a historian analyzing the past because they characterize a person whose own successes and failures are viewed within the continuum of human experience. Judgement is not the purpose of history for Marsden. Self-understanding is the purpose, self-understanding for the purpose of loving and understanding people made in the image of God.

The next chapter will examine how those within evangelical circles have received the kind of history being written by Noll, Hatch, and Marsden. To some extent, more implicitly, this next chapter will deal with the challenges scholarship raises for those who profess an evangelical Christian faith. The question of how one is to integrate faith and learning or whether an integration of the two is possible, is still a pressing issue in evangelical circles. Noll, Hatch, and Marsden are committed to the premise that evangelical Christians must integrate faith and scholarship if they are to have an influence on higher education. But they face charges from some in the evangelical community that they are accommodating to secular educational standards. The next chapter examines how they answer those charges and, in doing so, clarify their historical methods and interests. This chapter will also address the dilemma these conservative evangelical historians face when, in trying to be true to the dictates of good scholarship and provide a service to their own traditions, they end up transgressing cultural and theological boundaries within the evangelical community.

Notes

[1] Robert T. Handy, "Christian Faith and Historical Method: Contradiction, Compromise, or Tension?" in *History and Historical Understanding*, eds. C. T. McIntire and Ronald A. Wells (Grand Rapids: Wm. B. Eerdmans Publishing Company, 1984), 86-87.

[2] David W. Lotz, "A Changing Historiography: From Church History to Religious History," in *Altered Landscapes: Christianity in America, 1935-1985*, ed. David W. Lotz (Grand Rapids: Wm. Eerdmans Publishing Company, 1989) 314-318. See also Henry Warner Bowden," The Historiography of American Religion," in *The Encyclopedia of the American Religious Experience*, Vol. I eds. Charles H. Lippy and Peter W. Williams (New York: Charles Scribner's Sons, 1988), 3 ff. and *Church History in an Age of Uncertainty: Historiographical Patterns in the United States, 1906-1990* (Carbondale: Southern Illinois University Press, 1991).

[3] Ibid., 319-21

[4] Ibid., 324-28.

[5] Ibid., 330-337.

[6] Sydney E. Ahlstrom, "The Problem of the History of Religion in America," *Church History* 57 (1988): 136.

[7] Sydney Mead, "Church History in the Federated Schools," *Divinity School News* 20 (February 1953): 7.

[8] Mark Noll Interview, June 4, 1993.

[9] M. H. Interview, *Lucas*, 91.

[10] George A. Rawlyk, *Champions of the Truth: Fundamentalism, Modernism, and the Maritime Baptists* (Montreal&Kingston: McGill-Queens, University Press, 1990), 29.

[11] James D. Bratt, "The Dutch Schools," in *Reformed Theology in America*, ed. David F. Wells (Grand Rapids: Baker Book House, 1989), 20-21.

[12] M. H. Interview, *Lucas*, 93.

[13] Noll Interview, June 4, 1993. C. C. Goen challenged Noll's desire to be methodologically self-aware in his review of *The Gospel in America* edited by Noll, Hatch and John D. Woodbridge. Goen called the book historically exasperating, and criticized the editors for not differentiating between historical and confessional statements. He thought the book engaged in homiletical exhortation, referring to it as a "series of sermons based on history." C. C. Goen, review of *The Gospel in America: Themes in the Story of American Evangelicals*, John D. Woodbridge, Mark A. Noll, and Nathan O. Hatch, eds., In *Church History* 49 (December 1980): 478-79.

[14] Ibid.

[15] Ibid.

[16] Ibid.

[17] Ibid.

[18] Mark A. Noll, *A History of Christianity in the United States and Canada* (Grand Rapids: Wm. Eerdmans Pub. Comp., 1992), 1.

[19] Ibid., 3.

[20] M. H. Interview, *Lucas*, 95.

[21] Mark A. Noll, *Between Faith and Criticism* (Grand Rapids: Baker Book House, 1986), 6-9.

[22] Natch Interview #1, December 17, 1992

[23] Ibid.

[24] Nathan Hatch, "The Puzzle of American Methodism," Delivered as the Bartlett Lecture, Yale University, February 9, 1993, 4.

[25] Ibid., 9-10.

[26] Ibid., 10-11.

[27] Hatch Interview, December 17, 1992. Sir Herbert Butterfield's *The Whig Interpretation of History* (London: G. Bell and Sons, 1931) is the work which popularized this notion. For a more general treatment of the Whig interpretation of history see David Bebbington, *Patterns in History: A Christian Perspective on Historical Thought* (Grand Rapids: Baker Book House, 2nd edition, 1990).

[28] Nathan O. Hatch, *The Democratization of American Christianity* (New Haven: Yale University Press, 1989), 16.

[29] Ibid.

[30] Nathan O. Hatch, "Mormon and Methodist: Popular Religion in the Crucible of the Free Market," delivered as the O. C. and Grace Tanner Lecture, May 21, 1993, 12.

[31] Ibid., 17.

[32] Nathan Hatch, *The Sacred Cause of Liberty: Republican Thought and the Millennium in Revolutionary New England* (New Haven: Yale University Press, 1977).

[33] Bernard Bailyn, *History and the Creative Imagination* (St. Louis: Washington University Press, 1985), passim.

[34] Hatch Interview #2, June 3, 1993, at the University of Notre Dame.

[35] Carl L. Becker, "Detachment and the Writing of History" (1910), in *Detachment and the Writing of History: Essays and Letters of Carl L. Becker*, ed. P. L. Snyder (Ithaca: New York, 1958), 14.

[36] George Marsden, "Common Sense and the Spiritual Vision of History," in *History and Historical Understanding*, eds. C. T. McIntire and Ronald A. Wells (Grand Rapids: Wm. Eerdmans Pub. Comp., 1984), 56.

[37] Hatch Interview, December 17, 1992.

[38] Hatch Interview, June 3, 1993.

[39] Marsden Interview, June 3, 1993.

[40] Ibid.

[41] Ibid.

[42] Ibid.

[43] George Marsden, "A Christian Perspective for the Teaching of History," in *A Christian View of History?*, eds. George Marsden and Frank Roberts (Grand Rapids: Wm. Eerdmans Pub. Comp., 1975), 32. Mead, "Church History in the Federated Schools," 7.

[44] Ibid., 36.

[45] Sir Herbert Butterfield, *Christianity and History* (London: G. Bell and Sons, Ltd., 1949), 23-24.

[46] Ibid., 38-39.

[47] Ibid., 41.

[48] Ibid., 43-44.

[49] Leslie R. Keylock, "Evangelical Leaders You Should Know: Meet George Marsden," *Moody Monthly*, July/August 1986, 62.

[50] Marsden, *A Christian View of History*, 44.

[51] Ibid., 45.

[52] Ibid., 46.

[53] Ibid., 47-48.

3

Transgressing Boundaries: Historical Critique and Evangelical Response

On Friday, November 4, 1988 the Presbytery of the Free Presbyterian Church of Scotland, also known as the "Wee Frees," voted to suspend one of its elders. The suspension revoked his duties as an elder and banned him from receiving communion for six months. The reason for this disciplinary action concerned the elder's attendance at two Roman Catholic Requiem Masses. The "Wee Frees" followed a strict interpretation of the 1643 version of the Westminster Confession of Faith which described the Pope as the Anti-Christ and the Mass as idolatrous. Therefore, to attend a Mass was to break church law as defined by this version of the Westminster Confession of Faith.[1]

This story has significance because the elder in question was Lord Mackay, the Lord High Chancellor and highest ranking legal official in Britain. The Masses he attended were funerals for two law colleagues, both of whom were Catholic. Lord Mackay found himself in the difficult position of choosing between strict adherence to a faith commitment with clear doctrinal and cultural boundaries and the concern and loyalty that accompanied friendships developed in the secular legal world. In effect, he decided to transgress the doctrinal and cultural boundaries of the Free Presbyterian Church of Scotland in order to honor his deceased colleagues. In doing so he made a distinction between respect and advocacy. According to Lord Mackay, showing respect in attending a Mass for his professional colleagues was not advocating Catholicism.[2] Lord Mackay stood in two worlds at the same time. He was a lawyer and Lord High Chancellor of Great Britain and an elder in the Free Presbyterian Church. He did not see these two positions as mutually exclusive. There were, however, theological and sociological boundaries of permissible behavior established by his church. Once those boundaries were crossed, his two worlds were at odds.

In much the same way this chapter is about boundaries. It is about the various theological, academic, and cultural boundaries that ensure evangelical distinctives. These boundaries sometimes serve as litmus tests by which those in the evangelical community separate true evangelicals from those considered pseudo-evangelicals. Prohibitions among evangelicals against smoking, drinking, and dancing are sometimes institutionalized for the purpose of establishing these cultural boundaries. Other boundaries are more intellectual such as those found in evangelical education. Evangelical colleges and seminaries are known for asking their faculty to sign statements affirming certain theological tenets crucial to evangelical doctrine. In the case of the early years of Fuller Seminary, these confessions ranged from signing a statement affirming the Bible to be inerrant in the original autographs to refusing to support views associated with the National Council of Churches.

The 1940s and 50s witnessed the rise of neoevangelicalism led primarily by scholars such as Carl F. H. Henry and associated with the birth of Fuller Seminary in Pasadena, California. These scholars recognized the need for evangelicals to reclaim their intellectual heritage. Reclaiming this heritage, though, required them to overcome a fundamentalist stigma carried over from the late nineteenth-century.[3]

Fundamentalism in the late nineteenth-century was essentially characterized by an intense opposition to anything that smacked of modernism. Modernism included higher critical methods applied to Biblical research, the Darwinistic evolutionary hypothesis, Communism, socialism or anything else the fundamentalists identified as a threat to American culture. Because of their opposition to modernity, fundamentalists initially fought for control of mainline denominations in an attempt to preserve doctrinal orthodoxy. When this strategy proved unsuccessful, they shifted tactics and separated from their more liberal associates to form competing schools and agencies. In the process, fundamentalists also established certain theological and cultural boundaries designed to maintain the distinctives that clearly set them apart from those they saw as liberals and modernists. These boundaries were not always mutually agreed upon or universal in application among the many diverse fundamentalist groups. Rather, fundamentalists set up guidelines agreeable to their constituents and then chose to cooperate with other fundamentalists whose rules were similar. These boundaries tended to be decentralized and flexible and were often shaped to suit the agendas of fundamentalist leaders.[4]

Two examples of the decentralized and flexible nature of these boundaries can be found in the establishment of Westminster Seminary by J. Gresham Machen and a significant event in the early years of Fuller Seminary. Machen was a professor of New Testament at Princeton

Seminary who defended fundamentalism in his 1923 publication, *Christianity and Liberalism*. Because of his defense of fundamentalism, which was based largely on his view of Biblical inerrancy, Machen separated from Princeton Seminary in 1929 over the issue of doctrinal orthodoxy. He was initially joined by Carl McIntire. McIntire, along with Harold Ockenga and Francis Schaeffer, had been among those students who formed the first class at Westminster Seminary. Machen and McIntire agreed that Biblical inerrancy was a doctrinal distinctive that should mark all true evangelicals. They disagreed over the issue of whether a true Christian could smoke and drink. Because Machen was more moderate on these issues he considered adiaphora, McIntire separated from him to form a competing movement.[5]

Fuller Seminary was a stronghold for inerrancy and strictly conservative on issues like smoking and drinking. When Fuller hired Bela Vassady, McIntire attacked Fuller's decision because Vassady had been instrumental in the founding of the World Council of Churches (WCC). In McIntire's view, no true Christian could be involved in the WCC because the WCC promoted neo-orthodox theology along with liberal social and political views. Therefore, in McIntire's opinion, Fuller's decision to hire Vassady was tantamount to the seminary promoting neo-orthodoxy which in turn was a transgression of the theological boundaries essential to being a true evangelical and a true Christian.[6]

This separatist mentality tended to undermine the constructive processes of conflict resolution. Instead, it promoted a radical individualism that elevated personalities over truth. As a result, personalities were allowed to establish arbitrary boundaries which promoted increasingly divisive agendas. These boundaries eventually resulted in great strife among the faculty and supporters of Fuller Seminary. Proponents of a new and less divisive evangelical approach to scholarship, doctrine, and culture were opposed by those who felt that any movement away from a strict fundamentalist position in these areas was an abandonment of true Christianity. The tension of this struggle caused a former president of Fuller to write, "Fundamentalists defend the gospel, to be sure, but they sometimes act as if the gospel read, 'Believe on the Lord Jesus Christ, don't smoke, don't go to movies, and above all don't use the Revised Standard Version—and you will be saved.'"[7]

The events of the 1920s at Princeton and later at Fuller Seminary, designed to be a Princeton on the west coast, demonstrate how the evangelical world struggled in coming to terms with modernity and scholarship. Over the last forty years, this struggle has been carried on by the descendants of those early neoevangelicals who sought to reclaim an intellectual heritage for evangelicalism without surrendering their faith. Mark Noll, Nathan Hatch, and George Marsden, heirs of those early neoevangelicals, represent a significant block of evangelical historians. They are respected scholars who are conversant with the wider world of academics. They contribute to the dialogue and issues in their discipline, but they also seek to be true to their beliefs as Reformed evangelical Christians. As demonstrated in the last chapter, each of these men operates in two worlds. They are committed Christians with a Reformed perspective of faith and life, and they are professional historians. They do not believe their Christian beliefs are incompatible with their vocation because they believe academics are compatible with being a Christian. But all three speak in different ways of the tensions created when trying to hold academics and faith in balance while being true to both.

This chapter examines some of these tensions that take the form of cultural, theological, and academic boundaries. Most of the criticism and opposition faced by these historians comes from within evangelical ranks. The causes of this criticism vary. Some evangelicals are not happy with the way these historians view the early political and cultural history of America. Their historical views are seen as too secular. Other evangelicals do not like the term evangelical being applied to them, but, if it is, they want these historians to give their part of the evangelical story more credit or, at least, more emphasis.

Nathan Hatch spoke candidly about the kind of criticism he and others experienced as participants in the Institute for the Study of American Evangelicals. The next chapter will examine this organization more carefully, but all three of these men were instrumental in its founding. Hatch spoke of the criticism that they received from other evangelical scholars who questioned the openness they practiced in relating to scholars outside of evangelical circles. He went so far as to say that some within evangelical scholarship considered Noll, Marsden, and himself dangerous. Hatch said he was not sure why, but he felt that it was because other evangelicals wanted to define evangelicalism doctrinally and were therefore uncomfortable with historians who were not willing to draw careful theological lines.[8] Hatch said that after reflecting on this problem for several months he concluded:

> They see us as sort of too open. In this sort of evangelical world that
> doesn't have popes, councils, and creeds, the setting of boundaries
> is a difficult thing. The easiest way to be safe is to set boundaries.

Another way to be safe is to operate in a certain subculture, that's the way most evangelicals operate. The evangelical world is big enough so you can do that. It's therefore unnerving for them when those of us who claim evangelical convictions, transgress all these sociological boundaries, and mix it up in conferences, not always defining our distinctions.[9]

He went on to say that the separatist minded evangelicals of today were not afraid of losing influence in intellectual circles as evangelicals in the nineteenth century were. Hatch felt the separatists greatest fear was the slippery slope of accommodation that they identified with the demise of Harvard and Yale.[10]

It did bother Hatch when he heard other evangelicals criticize Noll and Marsden especially when Marsden was taking flack from scholars within the American Society of Church History who thought his presidential address was too evangelical. "That is what is hard, for evangelicals to say we are tremors, when to some extent we jeopardize our academic reputation for taking a firm stance. Transgression of boundaries is an important issue that characterizes almost everyone in this group. We are people who transgress boundaries."[11]

It is interesting to note that most of the serious criticism, at least to date, has come from within evangelical ranks and not from the more mainline members of the historical guild. This could mean that the mainline historians do not take these evangelical historians seriously, but this is doubtful since two of these evangelical historian have served successive terms as president of the American Society of Church History. Though the ASCH is dedicated primarily to religious and not secular historical studies, the same methods of doing history prevail there just as they does in other parts of the historical guild. The broader guild is aware of these historians but seems only to take real notice when one of them challenges the prevailing presuppositions of secular historiography such as the Enlightenment concept of value-free research. Marsden insists that Enlightenment concepts such as "value-free" research are no longer a valid basis for marginalizing a Christian worldview in academics. Chapter four will discuss these historians' views on the validity of a Christian worldview in higher education, and the criticism this position has drawn.

The Evangelical Historian and The Evangelist

The proper use and place of scholarship is a continuing source of misunderstanding and suspicion among evangelicals in this century. What should be the role of an evangelical Christian who strives for excellence in academics? If evangelicals are characterized by a mission of sharing the gospel of faith and repentance through Jesus Christ to a rebellious world, and if in order to accomplish this mission they must be different and separate from the values of the world they seek to convert to Christianity, then what role does scholarship play in this mission? Scholarship is usually characterized as being open to dialogue, different ideas, and values. By nature, scholarship is critical, and eschews approaches that are intolerant of other opinions, although it is often intolerant of those who do not meet its standards of tolerance. How does an evangelical scholar function as part of a community on mission to save a lost world, while at the same time contributing to a secular academic environment? This question sets the stage for a discussion and examination of this difficult dilemma as it finds expression in the scholarship of Marsden, Hatch and Noll.

The following discussion uses a specific set of correspondences and relationships as a means of illustrating a larger and more complex problem. It is not an attempt to cover everything pertinent to the problem raised in the previous paragraph, but it does provide insight into the tensions mentioned by Noll, Hatch, and Marsden when referring to the obstacles and criticisms of writing history as evangelicals. This chapter also provides insight into the thinking of other evangelicals who hold a different view of the purpose of scholarship and the role of a Christian scholar. One of the great benefits derived from studying this correspondence is clarification. Not only are historical and methodological positions more closely defined, but one is better able to understand how some evangelicals prioritize questions of Christian calling and ministry and their reasons for these priorities.

From November of 1982 to July of 1983, a significant amount of correspondence occurred between Francis A. Schaeffer, Mark Noll, and George Marsden. Schaeffer was part of Westminster Seminary's first graduating class. He went on to support Carl McIntire's separatist movement that left Westminster in the 1930s, but he later denounced his involvement in this movement because of its militant and divisive spirit. In the 1960s Schaeffer and his wife Edith founded a ministry called L'Abri in the Swiss mountains. L'Abri became a shelter to many young people searching for answers to religious questions in the turbulent 60s.

The correspondence between Schaeffer and Noll was precipitated by an article written by Kenneth L. Woodward and published in the November 1, 1982 issue of *Newsweek*. The article was entitled "Guru of Fundamentalism." The lively personal correspondence generated by this article eventually spilled over into the March 2, 1983 issue of The *Presbyterian Journal* where, for the next three months, it took on more the tone of a public debate as supporters on both sides had their say.[12]

Meanwhile, Marsden had been carrying on a correspondence with Francis Schaeffer that dated back to the 1960s. In 1967 Marsden visited Schaeffer's L'Abri ministry located outside of Huemoz, Switzerland. Marsden was attracted by Schaeffer's emphasis on the intellectual side of Christianity which took seriously the religious and cultural questions asked by many youth in the sixties. Marsden was both fascinated and frustrated by his time with Schaeffer. He found it difficult to penetrate what he described as a certain air surrounding Schaeffer's leadership of L'Abri. Schaeffer's approach inhibited Marsden from getting straight answers regarding the sources of Schaeffer's ideas.[13]

In 1968 Schaeffer was invited to speak at Calvin College where Marsden was teaching. The student response at Calvin was overwhelming as indicated by a front page article written for the underground student newspaper by Marsden in which he defended Schaeffer against attacks by some of the Calvin faculty, attacks that Marsden felt were unjustified considering the positive response of Calvin's student body.

> Not since the crowning of the Homecoming Queen was moved to Knollcrest has Franklin Auditorium been crowded with such an enthusiastic audience. With almost no promotional fanfare Mr. Francis Schaeffer of L'Abri Fellowship, Switzerland, accomplished what years of planned "Christian-hood," compulsory chapels, and "Religious Emphasis Weeks," as well as the efforts of a dedicated faculty, have seldom achieved at Calvin—perceptible enthusiasm for Christianity among the diverse elements of the student body.[14]

According to Marsden, most of the faculty at Calvin considered Schaeffer a charlatan and a pseudo-intellectual, but they could not deny the impact he had on the student body. Marsden defended Schaeffer's approach to cultural and theological issues, writing that for all his lack of academic credentials and standards, he did at least "make Christianity appear intellectually relevant to the contemporary era."[15] He applauded Schaeffer for demonstrating that is was possible to take seriously the thinking of the non-Christian secular world and to combine several different disciplines in order to present a more comprehensive Christian response to secular thought. In response to this article, Schaeffer told Marsden that he was one of the few people who understood him.[16]

The next significant communication between these two occurred in

1982. In February, Marsden wrote Schaeffer a two page letter in which he offered some historical observations on Schaeffer's recent book, *A Christian Manifesto*. These observations involved two basic critiques. First, Marsden suggested that Schaeffer could refine his historical arguments on the place of God's law in society. Schaeffer could accomplish this by being clearer in his understanding of the differences between the socio-political forms of the Protestant Reformation, especially those found in Calvinism, and the American Declaration of Independence and the Constitution. Marsden believed that the Declaration of Independence and the Constitution were based more on the principles of natural law. He felt that tying the Protestant Reformation too closely to the more secular legal principles reflected in the Constitution effectively weakened the distinction Schaeffer made between advocating the free exercise of religion as opposed to the type of theocracy the Puritans of Massachusetts sought to establish.[17]

The second observation pertained to a court case involving an Arkansas law that required the teaching of creation-science whenever the subject of origins was taught in public schools. This case had personal implications for Marsden because he served as an expert witness for those who opposed this law. He believed Schaeffer's reference to this case in his book was inaccurate. Schaeffer stated that the Arkansas law "allowed" the teaching of creation when the law stated that it was "required." Marsden believed there was a significant difference between the words "required" and "allowed." If the question was one of being allowed, then Marsden felt the case might conceivably be one of free exercise, but since the law required the teaching of creation-science, then the case was, in his opinion, one of establishment.[18]

Marsden went on to say that he felt his and Schaeffer's goals were not far apart. He appreciated Schaeffer's book as a "stirring call to action and to recognize the gravity of cultural-intellectual challenge—a cause to which I have been committed in my own work." Also, in a postscript, Marsden reminded Schaeffer of a previous letter in which Schaeffer lamented how evangelicals often substituted peripheral issues for real issues and therefore failed to make an impact. Marsden anticipated that Schaeffer would interpret his testifying in the Arkansas case as an example of majoring on minor issues. Having anticipated this response, Marsden defended his position with the comment that if evangelicals were to truly reclaim their society they must "establish complete credibility academically and intellectually, as Christians had done before the twentieth-century." He further wrote that in order to accomplish this task some evangelicals must be committed to making sharp distinctions as professional academicians. He acknowledged that the call of the academician was different from that of an evangelist but he felt that among believers the two should be seen as complementary even when seemingly at odds over certain issues.[19] Marsden believed that Christian callings could be different in function without being opposed in purpose. He thought it was possible to have differences and still be committed to the same goal.

Schaeffer responded to Marsden's letter with one of his own in April of 1982. In his response Schaeffer presented his views on the issues Marsden raised. Regarding Marsden's concern about the use of the Reformation, Schaeffer stood on the grounds that the Reformation was not perfect in what it accomplished in the social or political realms, but, when compared to what other worldviews had produced, the Reformation promoted a basis for law that reflected Christian principles. He believed it was significant that America was founded primarily by people from countries with a Reformation tradition. Thus, in Schaeffer's view, men like Benjamin Franklin consciously devised the political/legal system in the Constitution to operate under the premise that God was above the law.[20]

In regard to the Arkansas case, Schaeffer thought Marsden was wrong to join forces with groups like the American Civil Liberties Union in opposition to the creation-science law. Schaeffer's position was not tied to the Arkansas law per se but reflected a more general opposition to what he perceived as forces within American society dedicated to eliminating a viable Christian view from the public school system, politics, and the media. He believed these forces were arrayed against the teaching of creation-science in the Arkansas case, and therefore any cooperation with these forces was tantamount to assisting them in their overall agenda.[21]

Schaeffer commented on half of Marsden's postscript. He agreed that evangelicals had done damage to their cause for Christ by not recognizing the difference between crucial issues and marginal ones, but he did not elaborate on what issues were and were not crucial. He chose not to comment on Marsden's point regarding the difference between the task of an evangelist and a academician.

The specific historical issue raised by Marsden in this correspondence with Schaeffer and the more general issue regarding the distinct tasks of the academician and the evangelist were further defined and elaborated in the debate that ensued after the article about Schaeffer appeared in the November 1, 1982 issue of *Newsweek*. Mark Noll started this segment of the correspondence with a letter to Schaeffer on November 3. Generally, Noll wanted Schaeffer to know that, while he had been quoted correctly, he had not been quoted fully. He believed Schaeffer's work lacked the scholarship it needed in areas of historical accuracy, but, though he questioned some of Schaeffer's ideas, he was in concert with Schaeffer's efforts to call Christians to action. Noll echoed Marsden's conviction that Christians must be active in all areas of life, but Noll also agreed that Christians needed to exercise care and expertise in each of those areas.[22]

Under a separate addendum, Noll commented further on his uneasiness with Schaeffer's scholarship. Although he stood firmly with Schaeffer's overall Christian worldview, which depended on Dutch Calvinism in general and Abraham Kuyper specifically, Noll did not believe it was helpful for Schaeffer to call Christians to social or political action using unsound historical interpretations. Examples of such unsound interpretations included: the belief that the colonial and Revolutionary periods of America history were uniquely Christian periods of history and that the government of the United States was specifically biblical in its foundation. Noll felt that Christians should be called to action on the basis of sound biblical principles and insights rather than the shaky premise that America as a nation or a government was uniquely Christian. To illustrate his point, Noll referred to the poor track record of the United States government in defending the rights of Indians and slaves. Based on this past performance Noll stated that it would be wrong to use the nation's past as a rallying point for present action on issues of justice or morality.[23] In order to help Schaeffer in clarify these issues Noll sent him a copy of his recent essay, "The Bible in Revolutionary America."[24]

Schaeffer replied to Noll on November 20 in a letter intended as a response to all those in Noll's school of historical thought. Schaeffer's basic argument rested on the idea that the Founding Fathers were immersed in a society heavily influenced by a Christian consensus, and therefore, even though not all of these men were Christians, as he understood the term, their thinking and values were influenced by Christian thought and therefore, by implication, they were influenced by biblical thought. Schaeffer believed the difference between what the American Revolution produced and what the French Revolution produced was due to the Christian consensus that dominated eighteenth-century American society.

He listed errors he believed Christians made in thinking about America's early history. The first error was thinking that all the Founding Fathers were Christians, which Schaeffer believed was not valid. But equally invalid, in his mind, were those that used a proof-text method for determining if the Founding Father's political thinking was influenced by the Bible. He believed Noll's school of historical thought fell into this second error. It is interesting that in his argument against using a proof-text method, Schaeffer used himself as part of his argument. He in effect projected himself into the colonial past by stating that, had he been there, his thoughts would have been influenced directly by the Bible even if he failed to acknowledge that influence.

Schaeffer was especially dismayed by Noll's unwillingness to draw final conclusions where he thought the sources were uncertain. He felt this type of scholarship made Noll's research a negative influence in the work of mobilizing Christians to address pressing moral issues. Schaeffer was uncomfortable with admitting there was ambiguity in the historical record, and thus he was willing to overlook the lack of historical certitude in the sources for the sake of their immediate usefulness. He further felt that Noll's view of American history was an example of a more general evangelical conformity to secular society.[25]

A central problem or question that surfaced continually during the correspondence between Noll and Schaeffer was whether one could demonstrate the direct or indirect influence of the Bible in American history. How does one find and show evidence of Biblical influence in the historical sources? Both Schaeffer and Noll had similar goals. They wanted to use early American history as a tool to teach and inform evangelical Christians about their colonial heritage. But Noll wanted to inform evangelicals in order to correct historical interpretations like Schaeffer's, while Schaeffer wanted to inform evangelicals in order to prepare them for political action.

Schaeffer wanted the American past to serve as a motivation and foundation for mobilizing Christians for the battles of the present. America's colonial and Revolutionary history served this purpose if one could demonstrate that America was once a nation with a Christian consensus that resulted in laws based on Christian principles. If this argument could be supported, then the problems in America could be reduced to the idea that the nation had deviated from these early convictions. If this view truly represented the nation's past, then the leaders and events of American history could be used as examples for a present generation of Christians to emulate. The past could then serve as a rallying point for believers in America to reclaim the nation's Christian heritage.

Noll wanted American history to reflect the good and bad, the righteousness and sinfulness of the Christian story in America. He wanted to avoid a triumphal history that placed Christians, particularly Protestant

Christians, on a pedestal. If the past was to be useful for the evangelical community then it must be allowed to speak the truth, and if the truth was dim and unclear or not complimentary then one must avoid the temptation of embellishing it to make it more palatable for Christian consumption. Certainly there were those people and events that demonstrated the best of the Christian community and one should be thankful for those who lived exemplary lives. On the other hand, Noll's Augustinian view of human nature and his study of the historical sources taught him to accept the fact that people fail even in their best intentions. If the past was to be helpful in answering the questions of the present, then Christians in the present must take seriously the failures of Christians throughout history.

In his response to Schaeffer's critique of his work, Noll tried to be precise about the criteria he used in determining biblical influence on the founders. He clarified that he was not looking for proof-texts from the Bible in the sources but rather he was searching for two things: (1) was there an apparent conviction that human groups, even those in the "new world," were crippled by sin and needed to feel the effects of redemption,[26] and (2) was there a conviction that God's specific and gracious providence undergirded political life, and not simply nature or human nature.

Noll felt the sources did not indicate that the founders had a specifically biblical base for their political convictions. In fact, Jefferson and Franklin conspicuously avoided the use of Scriptural authority and Madison was often ambiguous in his views on the Bible. Even John Witherspoon, who was an evangelical, set aside the Bible when he spoke about political issues. It was John Witherspoon who received most of Noll's attention because Noll found in Witherspoon a good example of how a Christian could set aside his biblical beliefs when entering secular affairs and thus pave the way for secular thinking to dominate social and political life. Thus, in Noll's view, even though Witherspoon was an evangelical Christian, he was not a good example for Christians to follow in reclaiming their society for Christ. Noll used, in this instance, a favorite phrase of Schaeffer in explaining his case. He wrote that Witherspoon, in his approach to politics, made it possible for nature to "eat up grace." He further wrote that evangelicals today still struggled with Witherspoon's mentality, a mentality that resulted in evangelicals leaving their Christian worldview at the door along with their hat and coat before entering the day's business.[27]

Noll went on to say that evangelicals in the eighteenth and nineteenth-centuries adopted an uncritical view of themselves and their culture that eventually led them to believe that American culture was essentially

Christian. Thus they were unprepared for the tumultuous intellectual challenges of the late nineteenth-century that shook the foundations of what was considered to be an American culture dominated by conservative Protestantism. Evangelicals erred by identifying conservative Protestantism with American culture. Therefore, when the intellectual climate of the culture changed, evangelicals found themselves on the outside, dazed and struggling for respect and recognition from the very educational institutions they helped to establish.[28]

Noll compared this situation with that of Holland during the same period. Men like Abraham Kuyper recognized that in spite of the strength of evangelical Christianity, the church stood in opposition to much of what was happening in Dutch culture. In response to that situation, Kuyper helped found the Free University of Amsterdam to provide a place for Christian thinking to be applied to the social, political, educational, and intellectual challenges of Dutch culture. This kind of critical thinking, however, was not active among American evangelicals of the same period. Noll's point was that a true reading of history should include both weaknesses and strengths if evangelicals in the present were to avoid the same pitfalls. In summary, Noll wrote that his view of American history, "will not seek Christian political principles for the modern world from the founders or think that valued Christian action will arise from the compromising history of American evangelical culture."[29]

In his letter of December 20, 1982, Schaeffer offered a solution to the impasse between himself and Noll. Although he still felt Noll was wrong in his view of American history, he had hopes that they could find common ground based on the nature/grace model referred to by Noll. Schaeffer's solution was to think of the past in terms of a spectrum. At one end of the spectrum he placed Kuyper with his unified view of the Christian life as opposed to the nature/grace separation. Schaeffer believed Kuyper was correct in his view that the nature/grace separation was a destructive mentality. On the other end of the spectrum Schaeffer placed the results of the French and Russian Revolutions where autonomous reason was substituted for a Creator. Schaeffer then suggested that other people and ideas be placed on this spectrum based upon how closely they resembled one end or the other. He placed Jefferson closer to the French Revolution and Witherspoon closer to Kuyper but he placed both men close to the middle based upon his belief that Jefferson and Witherspoon at least shared the idea of a Creator. This idea that the founders shared a common view of a Creator was evidently sufficient for Schaeffer as proof of biblical influence. He believed that when the Christian influence of that century was compared to subsequent centuries, a gradual decline of that influence could be demonstrated. This decline suggested to Schaeffer that a stronger Christian consensus did exist in the eighteenth-century. This influence, in his opinion, surely affected the founder's political beliefs. Schaeffer spent the remainder of the letter arguing that those who did not write and teach history in a way that clearly demonstrated a biblical and Christian influence on the Founding Fathers of the nation were remiss. In effect, Schaeffer felt that this kind of historical research contributed to the further decline of American culture by assisting those forces intent on diminishing a significant Christian voice in American society and politics. He ended the letter by stating he intended to send copies of it to those he felt would be helped by its contents.[30]

In turn, Noll sent a copy of Schaeffer's letter to George Marsden who wrote Schaeffer in January of 1983. Marsden took it upon himself to refute what he perceived as a misunderstanding on Schaeffer's part regarding the motives of those "conservative Reformed historians" who were writing history from a historical-critical position. Marsden took issue with Schaeffer's suggestion that when these conservative Reformed historians questioned the Christian character of America's founders they were, in effect, furthering or contributing to the secular cultural values of the twentieth-century. Marsden countered that their purpose was accuracy in explaining the strengths and weaknesses of American culture and the nature of its relationship with evangelicalism. Unless evangelicals understood their own tradition and its relationship to the culture, how could they hope to fight intelligently the prevailing values and ideas of that culture?[31]

Marsden further argued that it was not valid for Schaeffer to suggest that even their best intentions were playing into the hands of those seeking a secular society void of Christian influence. Marsden reminded Schaeffer that one cannot always be responsible for the irresponsible ways others use their work. For Marsden, the crucial thing was not whether one's work was being misused, but rather, was one telling the truth? "Consequences of what one might say should, of course, be taken into account; but the crucial thing to seek is to get things right. Otherwise we will be left with a pragmatic standard for what we say—a result that you lament in other contexts. So we can not tailor our historical generalizations just to suit the needs of the moment—even if they be urgent needs."[32]

Marsden was convinced that a lack of accuracy in understanding and describing the past only contributed to a distorted view of history and consequently a distorted perspective on how history assists in understanding the present. He did not agree that understanding the forces of atheism present in the French and Russian Revolutions was enough; one must also see and admit that those forces are also an inherent part of American culture as well. Marsden emphasized the importance of being able to distinguish between what he felt was Christian or biblical and what was cultural.[33]

Mark Noll wrote a letter to Schaeffer in January of 1983 in which he listed five points of agreement and four points of disagreement. The areas of agreement tended to be more theological in nature and included: the need for a more unified Christian worldview; the value of Kuyper in this regard; the weakness of evangelicals on this issue; the problem the Enlightenment brings to having a unified worldview; and the need to let Scripture rule over all of life.[34] These areas of agreement were possible because both men were indebted to a strong Calvinistic theology.

The areas of disagreement were historical. Noll did not believe that the deeply secular nature of American society was a recent occurrence. He believed it was rooted in the early years of the Republic and the failure of the founders, who were Christians, to employ Christian thinking in their political views. This failure led to the dominance of Enlightenment thought. Refusing to recognize this fact of history led modern evangelicals to adopt an uncritical view of the Founding Fathers as models for modern political and social action. In Noll's view, this kind of unthinking activism perpetuated the nature/grace separation that existed during the Revolution because it baptized a quasi-historical view of the nation's founding, a founding that was a mixture of Christian and Enlightenment thought.[35]

It was at this point in time that the debate turned more public. G. Aiken Taylor, editor of The *Presbyterian Journal*, published an editorial in the March 2 edition entitled "Francis Schaeffer: America's Historical Underpinnings," in which he defended Schaeffer's historical views by calling upon C. Gregg Singer, another church historian, to provide support for those views.[36] This editorial was answered in turn by George Marsden and Henry F. Lazenby in the March 30 edition. Marsden pointed out that even Singer at another time had admitted that the Declaration of Independence, signed by Witherspoon and others, had an "anti-Christian character."[37] Lazenby offered his knowledge of Witherspoon from research he did for his doctorate at Aberdeen University in Scotland. Witherspoon, he wrote, did indeed lay aside the Bible when approaching politics because his views on human nature and the nature of politics were based on the Scottish Common Sense Philosophy of Thomas Reid, not the Bible.[38]

There was further correspondence of this type among Marsden, Noll, and Schaeffer, but what has been shared thus far is representative of the remaining letters. There is no need to belabor the point that these men were separated by serious differences in their view of American history. An examination of the letters written between March and July of 1983 shows an impasse had been reached that was never bridged. While Marsden's and Noll's letters remained consistent in their attempt to clarify problems raised about specific historical issues, Schaeffer's letters became increasingly redundant. By this time, Schaeffer had identified the work of Noll, Marsden, and others like them as a definite historical school of thought that he disliked. The principle areas of difference between Noll, Marsden, and Schaeffer were historical, but there was also an implicit area of difference regarding the role and task of the historian and the evangelist.

Once they placed the historical questions on the table for discussion, expressed their views on these questions, and responded to each other's views, the conversation shifted. It became clear that the historical questions were not going to be answered to everyone's satisfaction, but the debate continued. Almost imperceptibly, however, the grounds of the discussion changed from questions of historical perspective to questions of motives, agendas, one's value to the evangelical community, the urgent need for evangelical action in pinpointing the "real issues," and not playing academic games.

Schaeffer became increasingly concerned that these historians were sacrificing what was needed to rally evangelicals to reclaim the nation for Christ (i.e. a vision of America as formerly a Christian nation), for historical accuracy. Thus his position on the historical issues went unchanged. Instead he appealed to Noll and Marsden to take seriously the moral and ethical state of the nation and not to let their historical work dull the urgent need for evangelicals to unite in reclaiming America for Christ. Schaeffer felt Noll and Marsden majored on minor issues by insisting that the call for political action should not rest on the example of the nation's founders. The real issues for Schaeffer were abortion, free speech, prayer in the public schools, and evangelical involvement in the political process—not historical accuracy. These issues were all signs that the nation had drifted from God and needed to be called back. Schaeffer was fulfilling his role as an evangelist and a prophet. It was his calling and task to address the immediate issues and get action from the evangelical community.

The issues that concerned Schaeffer also concerned Noll and Marsden. Their letters offered encouragement to him as he faced these crucial issues.

But, unlike Schaeffer, they were not evangelists. They were historians. While they felt the issues were vital and called for action, they would not sacrifice a truthful narrative of the nation's past in order to provide a pragmatic means to rally evangelical support. They were convinced that the Bible was the proper place to gain instruction and guidance for the action Schaeffer wanted. The role of Christians in American history was only useful if one could differentiate between the thinking and choices that were biblical and those that followed the prevailing secular thought of that day. To confuse the two by uncritically following a syncretistic mix of political language and religious rhetoric only perpetuated the problem of separating truly Christian thinking from secular. It was at this level of making the distinctions and recognizing the differences, that these historians saw themselves making their contribution to evangelical life. They were committed to engaging the intellectual and academic world and challenging its prevailing secular worldview, but, in order to do this, they could not afford to make historical judgements that were wrong, even for the sake of urgent needs.

This is where the tension lay and the rub came between evangelist and historian. Schaeffer's emphasis on the urgent moral, ethical, and political demands of the moment were weighed in the balance against Noll's and Marsden's insistence that historical accuracy and intellectual integrity must not be sacrificed in the name of activism. As an evangelist, Schaeffer felt these historical interpretations hindered his efforts at calling evangelicals to action. In a letter to Noll in March of 1983 he complained of an article in the *Reformed Journal* written by Ronald Wells. Schaeffer thought this article undercut the Reformation's emphasis on biblical truth and its significance for western history. He connected Wells with the historical school of thought that included Noll and Marsden, and suggested that they should be active in preventing such views from being expressed.[39]

In his book, The *Great Evangelical Disaster*, under the subtitles, "The Devaluation of History" and "Academic Infiltration," Schaeffer expressed these thoughts on Wells' article and the general state of evangelical scholarship.

> But there are those within evangelical circles today who would, under the guise of scholarship, belittle all of this and act as though the Christian consensus was always in a total muddle. Just how far this can be taken may be shown by the example of one Christian historian who carries the muddle all the way back to the Reformation itself. . . . What we have here is the infiltration of thoroughly secularized thinking presented as if it were evangelical scholarship.[40]

Schaeffer then praised younger evangelicals for initially rejecting a confined view of spiritual and intellectual life, but he felt they had ultimately gone awry.

Many young evangelicals heard this message, went out into the academic world, and earned their undergraduate and graduate degrees from the finest secular schools. But something happened in the process. In the midst of totally humanistic colleges and universities, and a totally humanistic orientation in the academic disciplines, many of these young evangelicals began to be infiltrated by the anti-Christian worldview which dominated the thinking of their college professors. In the process, any distinctively evangelical point of view was accommodated to the secularistic thinking in their discipline and to the surrounding world spirit of our age. To make the cycle complete, many of these have now returned to teach at evangelical colleges where what they present in their classes has very little that is distinctively Christian.[41]

These sentiments echoed Schaeffer's concerns about the teaching and writing of Noll and Marsden. In fact, these sentiments are reminiscent of Noll's observation about the sons and daughters of evangelicals who go off to the university with well wishes and pride, but who return as unwelcome scholars when they question the values of that community or suggest the need for changes.

The greater weight of this correspondence indicates that there are intellectual boundaries within the evangelical community, and, though these boundaries are often undefined and unspoken, they exist nonetheless. It also appears that the language of academic discussion and research is awkward and cumbersome for those evangelicals who harbor a certain amount of suspicion toward the world of scholarship. Schaeffer placed a high priority on Christian thinking and the development of a total worldview, and did much to promote these themes in an evangelical community that had almost abandoned the life of the mind. But, when faced with moral and ethical issues that cried out for Christian action, he became impatient, critical, and suspicious of evangelical historians who insisted that the urgency of the moment was not an excuse for intellectual shortcuts or poor scholarship. At this point, it seemed to Schaeffer that these historians were playing intellectual games, thereby accommodating to the secular academic world. Schaeffer remained true to his calling as an evangelist, a call that demanded immediate, and urgent action. This calling was so intense he could not accept Noll's and Marsden's calling as historians and scholars.

Marsden spoke to these differences in calling in a letter to Schaeffer in May of 1983. Marsden wrote of his agreement with Schaeffer regarding the goal of permeating the culture with a distinctly Christian worldview. Marsden also agreed that the battle was "first of all spiritual" and that it involved "at very deep levels ideologies and worldviews that permeate and shape cultures." But it was at this point that Marsden found gaps in their acceptance of each other's strategies. Marsden saw the world of scholarship as the place where, as a Christian, he engaged the worldviews of the day "at the highest level of scholarship that I can participate in." He was encouraged that this call to engage the academic world, which included other evangelical scholars, was having some results "in important centers of Western learning." Marsden wrote that his involvement in academics was a ministry just as Schaeffer's work at L'Abri was a ministry, though of a different type. He further emphasized that if evangelical scholars were to continue to have a positive impact on the minds and hearts of those they associated with in the academic world, they must continue to be careful and rigorous in their scholarship. If they abandoned this type of approach for the sake of promoting a cause, no matter how important, they would not only lose the academic integrity they had gained but, more importantly, the things that were important and needed to be heard would fall on deaf ears. He lamented the fact that there were evangelicals not doing their homework on certain issues with the result that, no matter how right their cause was, they were disregarded by the very people who could make a difference. Thus, instead of providing something serious for skeptics to consider, "you are just left preaching to the converted."[42]

In this same year, Nathan Hatch joined Marsden and Noll to co-author a book entitled, The *Search for Christian America*. They wrote the book as a general corrective for a less critical, evangelical view of America's past that identified evangelical Christianity with America's colonial history. More specifically, however, the book was a response to Schaeffer. In the introduction, the authors stated their essential argument. America never had a golden age in which the principles of Scripture were reflected in an ideal society. In fact, evangelicals should assume some of the blame for the secular nature of American society. Further, the idea of "a Christian nation" is opposed by the greater weight of Christian teaching because it hinders, not helps, effective Christian service in society.[43]

In chapter six, Marsden addressed this second part of the argument. Marsden challenged the idea that a proper and successful political or social agenda could be established upon the false notion that America had a uniquely Christian past. His argument was presented as a syllogism: if it is true that early America was a mixture of Christian and non-Christian influences; and if we fail to qualify this mixture by calling it "biblical," "Reformation-based," or Christian; then the impression is left that the authority of God's Word is, in effect, syncretistic at its heart. The result is confusion on the part of evangelicals who are unable to distinguish what is cultural from what is evangelical in the nation's heritage. Consequently, these evangelicals end up basing their strategy to reclaim the nation on grounds that are neither historical nor biblical.[44]

Nathan Hatch contributed chapter seven in which he warned against four defective views of history. He warned against seeing the past as a mirror because this view often mistakes the echo of its own voice for the wisdom of the past. The past should also not be a place of escape because in doing so people disparage their own tradition as if it had nothing to offer. By failing to understand their own tradition, they end up being unconsciously shaped by it. The past was not a golden age to be recaptured. Setting the past up as a standard for judging the actions of the present establishes a false ideal that discourages action. It gives the impression that God is not as interested or involved in the present as he was in the past, and that the present generation of Christians will never measure up to those in the past. Finally, the past was never an orderly chain of cause and effect. As a result, studying the past is not a simple exercise of sorting out the good and bad. Both good and bad are mixed and shaken together. We are able to see both good and bad, but the sequence of events in the past does not always make it clear as to how or why these elements took the forms they did. Hatch did not believe that the complexities of history should ever be an excuse for inaction in the present, but rather, he hoped to aid Christians in their quest for truth by dispelling several mistaken notions of history as a warning against using unwarranted historical judgements in support of Christian causes.[45]

Was this book successful in correcting the defective historical understanding the authors saw among evangelicals? In specific terms it did not change Schaeffer's position on the historical questions debated through his lengthy correspondence with these historians. When everything was said and done, he still felt that admitting to a less than an evangelical consensus among the founders of the nation was giving away too much, and jeopardized the success of a concerted effort to turn the tide of secular dominance in American society.

In general terms there is no indication that the historical views that characterized Schaeffer's work have diminished in popularity or use among evangelicals. Evangelicals still show an affinity for coupling the flag and the gospel as a dual symbol of a national heritage now lost. *The Search for a Christian America* was written with the assumption that evangelicals were critical of their beliefs and could be persuaded to test the historical assumptions of those beliefs.

Randall Balmer's book, *Mine Eyes Have Seen the Glory*, demonstrated, on a grassroots level, something that Nathan Hatch has written about extensively. Christianity in America has been democratized. The nation's history has been blended with biblical beliefs to produce a religious hybrid of democratic sentiments and biblical values which unite to form a religious ethos peculiar to this nation. This ethos is particularly evident among evangelical groups because of a lack of critical thinking. There is a separation, a wide gulf, between the popular court of religious opinion that drives most evangelical communities of faith and the halls of academic authority where ideas and beliefs are analyzed and evaluated. Christian action within these evangelical communities is driven more by perception and opinion than the facts of scholarship.[46]

Noll, Marsden, and Hatch found themselves in the difficult position of struggling as scholars to provide a helpful historical corrective against the tide of popular evangelical opinion about America's origin on the one hand, while, on the other hand, defending themselves against the accusation that their commitment to scholarship and historical precision meant they were selling out the cause of evangelicalism. This section was entitled "The Evangelical Historian and the Evangelist" because the two functions are different, but the question is, does difference in this case mean distance? After reviewing these letters and other sources of the argument, one is left with the impression that it is okay for evangelicals to be scholars as long as they remember they must submit their scholarship for approval at the higher court of evangelical opinion. There is also the feeling that the whole idea of serious evangelical scholarship is, at times, an uncomfortable concept for many evangelicals who are more pragmatic in their strategies for personal and social change. At least in this exchange between Noll, Marsden, and Schaeffer, the distance and difference between the evangelical historian and the evangelist is significant.

Holiness or Reformed: Which Paradigm?

Another critique of these historians comes from within the ranks of the holiness tradition. The primary source of this critique is Donald Dayton, Professor of Theology and Ethics at Northern Baptist Theological Seminary. Dayton's own background was Wesleyan Methodist. He was educated at Wheaton College, Columbia University, Yale Divinity School, and received his doctorate from the University of Chicago. His dissertation was published in 1988 under the title, *The Theological Roots of Pentecostalism.*[47]

Dayton's critique of these historians has one major point with two corollaries. His primary point is historiographical in nature and can be summarized by his phrase, "the Presbyterianization of evangelical historiography."[48] By this he means that Marsden, Noll, Hatch, and other evangelical historians who adhere to a Reformed position, have forced a paradigm upon the history of evangelicalism in America that is Reformed in theology, linked directly to Princeton and the liberal/conservative fights over doctrine, associated with the rise of fundamentalism in response to the threat of modernity, and guilty of defining modern evangelicalism in these terms.

The first of his corollaries concerns the word "evangelical." Dayton believes that the immense amount of diversity present among those who call themselves evangelicals far out weighs any commonalties. He agrees that on the surface movements such as pentecostalism and fundamentalism seem to share a common understanding of Scripture. They both appear to use the Scriptures in a very strict, literal sense. However, Dayton sees a significant difference in the pentecostal approach which he calls a "precritical" approach to Scripture and what he terms the "anticritical" approach of fundamentalism.[49] In other words pentecostalism operates with a theological understanding of Scripture that is not conversant with the higher critical methods that create such controversy among fundamentalists. Fundamentalists intentionally reject the theological methodology of higher criticism. He thus concludes that whatever alliances were formed in the National Association of Evangelicals during the 1940s between pentecostal/charismatic groups and the more orthodox conservative churches were designed to create a power base for neoevangelicals in their ecclesiastical struggles. But in time these alliances dissolved, showing that the historical and theological rational for their formation was too weak to maintain. Dayton attributed this breakup to the significant differences that existed initially but were overlooked. Therefore he contends that the word evangelical should be dropped altogether as he feels it no longer communicates anything distinct or definable.[50]

The second corollary is his contention that the true stream of American evangelicalism that emerged from the late nineteenth-century was radical, revivalist, reform conscious, anti-mainline, anti-status quo, and grassroots in its make-up. He associates this revised mainstream with holiness and perfectionist groups that tended to be more pragmatic and experimental than creedal and orthodox. He describes this movement of radical, reform-minded Christians as representing non-traditional Christianity, a modern, radical version of Christianity. In this radical version of Christianity Dayton finds his own sense of mission and calling. "The radicalism that I would share with both finds reverberation in the complaints of the 'radical reformation' against the magisterial reformation, in the evangelical 'call to seriousness' over against the nominal Christianity of the 18th century, in the attack of Soren Kierkegaard on the state-church 'Christendom' of the 19th century, and in Bonhoeffer's complaints about 'cheap grace' in the recent past, and in the emergence of a 'radical evangelicalism' in our own day."[51]

In 1976 Dayton published, *Discovering an Evangelical Heritage.* The purpose of the book was to call evangelicals back to a heritage that Dayton believed they had abandoned. He wrote out of a conscious sense of his own personal struggles in reconciling his evangelical upbringing with the social and political issues of the tumultuous sixties. Dayton's basic premise was that true evangelicalism emerged from the revivalist movements of the nineteenth-century before the rise of fundamentalism. He used his book to marshal significant historical evidence that the true mainstream of evangelicalism in America came from radical, reform minded revivalists who established movements and institutions designed to make changes in the structure of American society.[52] Dayton meant for this interpretation of evangelicalism to stand in opposition to what he saw as the prevailing view which pictured modern evangelicalism as emerging from the Fundamentalist/ Modernist fights of the nineteenth-century, and the theological influence of Princeton Seminary.

In chapter ten he asked what happened to the reform impulse that characterized the evangelicalism described in his book. What happened to the desire for reform that motivated Theodore Weld, the Tappan brothers, and others to found colleges that supported the cause of abolition and social change? One reason he gave for the loss in the evangelical impulse towards was the shift in theology among revivalists after the Civil War. Those before the war were postmillennialist, those after the war were premillennialist. Premillennialism undercut the social reform movement in evangelicalism as it emphasized separation from a sinful world and a generally anti-cultural mentality. Dayton believed this theological shift was exacerbated by the growing influence among evangelicals of Old School Presbyterianism located at Princeton Seminary. Princeton theology was opposed to revivalism, emphasized right doctrine over right behavior, and was conservative in its social views. Dayton connected the rise of premillennialism and the Princeton theology with the decline of evangelical social involvement. He thus concluded that these two influences led to the loss of an evangelical heritage.[53]

In his epilogue Dayton made his case for the difference between the holiness, reform paradigm and the Reformed, orthodox paradigm for evangelicalism. Basically he saw the holiness model as pre-dating the Reformed model. Thus, he believed that it better represented American evangelicalism. He attributed the present use of the term evangelical to second generation Fundamentalists in the 1940s who called themselves evangelicals in order to create a more positive image of themselves. He characterized these neoevangelicals as emphasizing right doctrine and orthodoxy, while the nineteenth-century evangelicals focused more on the efficacy of grace that precedes the "new life" of the believer. Dayton believed this focus on "new life" energized the evangelical reform movements of that century.[54]

George Marsden reviewed Dayton's book in the *Christian Scholar's Review*. He found the book helpful in its call for social action on the part of evangelicals and in the solid historical resources used, but he disagreed with the premise and conclusion of the book. Marsden felt that Dayton had overstated his case concerning those who represented the radical reform of the nineteenth-century. He pointed out that Methodism split over the issue of social reform because of the social conservatism of its membership. He went on to point out that most of nineteenth-century evangelicalism was in fact socially conservative, and that this label of being socially status quo was not exclusively the right of Old School Presbyterians. Marsden also challenged the radical aspect of those Dayton chose as examples of evangelical reform by pointing out that these same people also promoted reactionary movements such as anti-masonry and anti-Catholicism. Furthermore, Marsden felt that Dayton understated the conversionist mentality of the reformers he mentioned. Conversion of the individual was seen as the necessary step in achieving a broader social reform. Social reform was the needed by-product but not the goal of these reformers. Marsden also saw more kinship between holiness and fundamentalist groups in that they both tended to be the offspring of nineteenth-century evangelicals who were more sectarian and radical in their cultural attitudes.[55]

In a 1991 article written for *Church History*, Douglas Sweeney explored these two competing paradigms of evangelical history, concluding that neither one told the whole story. Both were needed if evangelicals were to make sense out of their present identity crisis.[56] Coming to terms with the exact nature and makeup of present day evangelicalism seems to be a ongoing problem for those who consider themselves part of that community. No one wants to be slighted when the story is told but the question is, which story will be told? Even efforts at picturing evangelicalism have been diverse. Timothy Smith sees it as a kaleidoscope, Randall Balmer prefers the image of a patchwork quilt, while George Marsden has referred to it as an evangelical denomination.

Sweeney may have hit on something when he called this historiographical problem an observer-participant dilemma. Each party in this debate is only able to be an observer-participant from their portion of the evangelical tradition, and while both recognize that each tradition played a part in evangelical history, both parties are frustrated by the inability of the other to understand the uniqueness of their position. For example, George Marsden, commenting on the need to be self-critical, said, "Don Dayton doesn't understand that writing about a certain tradition does not mean we are celebrating it."[57] Dayton felt equally misunderstood. Recounting the particulars of a meeting with Marsden in 1988 he wrote, "He (Marsden) describes as a "fruitful exchange" what I experienced as a nearly unmitigated fiasco."[58]

This historiographical debate between Dayton and Marsden, which *Christian Scholar's Review* covered in 1977, was continued in the September 1993 issue. The essence of the discussion was essentially the same as that in the 1977 issue with the exception that this time the topic for discussion was Marsden's *Reforming Fundamentalism*, and they were joined in their discussion by Joel Carpenter, Dan Fuller, Clark Pinnock, and Douglas Sweeney.

In his critique, Dayton essentially remained true to his conviction that evangelical historiography was dominated by a Presbyterian theological paradigm. He felt that his examination of Marsden's institutional history of Fuller Seminary was further proof of his contention that a Presbyterian theological paradigm existed. Dayton believed that Marsden suppressed evidence that the founders of Fuller Seminary were products of holiness teaching and influence, and that Fuller's pre-history and founding should be understood from a holiness paradigm and not a Calvinistic one. As evidence for this theory Dayton produced research on the life and beliefs of one of Fuller's primary founders, Harold Ockenga. Dayton argued that Ockenga was not in line with "Old Princeton" theology but was instead a "closet Methodist." To substantiate this assertion, he recounted Ockenga's Methodist/holiness background, his years of pastoring Methodist churches, and excerpts from Ockenga's sermons which emphasized holiness themes, and utilized Keswickian language. Dayton also pointed out the pentecostal and holiness connections of another founder, Charles Fuller. He then summarized his research on the holiness background of Fuller Seminary by pointing out that many of its initial faculty members were speakers at a holiness/pentecostal camp meeting in New England. Dayton referred to the New England Fellowship which operated this camp as the "womb of the National Association of Evangelicals."⁵⁹

In another line of argument for his holiness paradigm, Dayton challenged the idea that modern evangelicalism was a result of a conservative/liberal fight within mainline denominations. Instead, he opted for the view that the splits in mainline churches like the Presbyterian Church in the 1930s were sociological not theological. He called these splits, the "embourgeoisment" of evangelicalism. He associated this embourgeoisment with the movement of some evangelicals toward more radical, open views of theology and society and away from the theological and sociological orthodoxy in mainline churches. In Dayton's opinion, the splits that purveyors of a Presbyterian model have associated with a conservative reaction to modernity were actually the result of internal struggles between evangelicals who sought a more radical approach to Christian living and the prevailing conservative status quo within the church. He classified these radical evangelicals as the true children of the reform minded evangelicals of the nineteenth-century.⁶⁰

Dayton also believed that this process of embourgeoisment was the explanation for why many evangelicals, especially those at Fuller, distanced themselves from dispensationalist teachings as they moved closer to the centers of social and theological power. Dayton described embourgeoisment as a process. Embourgeoisment begins with the lower classes who form new religious movements in order to infuse a dying faith with new energy, but upward social mobility moves these people into the middle class where they interact with the centers of social power. Thus, now removed from the social fringe, they want a more significant part in the social order and so they sacrifice their zeal for reform for a share of the power. Dayton believes this is what the neoevangelicals at Fuller did with dispensationalism when it became a barrier to what they wanted to achieve. He thus believes that dispensationalism played a larger role in the story of fundamentalism and the rise of neoevangelicalism at Fuller than Marsden indicates or wants to admit.⁶¹

In response, Marsden wrote that he disagreed with Dayton's two paradigm concept. He believed that Dayton's "Presbyterian paradigm" was not a useful historical model, and thus not one he would use. Marsden failed to see what Dayton found objectionable about his book in terms of his portrayal of the historical background leading to the founding of Fuller Seminary. Marsden agreed with Dayton that the founders were in fact broader interdenominational evangelicals with more roots in the "New School" Presbyterianism than in the "Old School" Princeton theology. He also believed that "the 'New School' Presbyterian evangelicalism and its Baptist counterparts were the most important precedents for early Fuller." Marsden reiterated that he did not say that the founders were in the tradition of the "Old School" Princeton, but rather, that they thought they were or wanted to be.[62]

In Marsden's view Dayton was too concerned with the question of orthodoxy. Dayton's over concentration on the problem of defining evangelicalism in orthodox terms led him to deemphasize the significance of defending orthodoxy against theological liberalism. Subsequently, in Dayton's revision of the story, the element of anti-modernism would be absent from the history of fundamentalism. In writing the Fuller history Marsden attempted to tell the story through the eyes of men like Carl Henry, Harold Lindsell, Wilbur Smith and others. "All these men had deep concerns with 'orthodoxy' and with presenting an intellectually respectable traditional Christianity that would answer modernism and secularism."[63] Marsden pointed out that it was these men as the characters of the story and not himself as the historian, "who tended to suppress aspects of the 'pentecostal' side of their heritage. By describing the important features of the history the way they saw it, I am not thereby endorsing their view. I am only describing it."[64] Marsden also pointed out that Dayton bemoaned the fact that the founder of Gordon-Conwell Seminary taught faith healing, but that today one can only teach on its faculty if he or she is in "the line of Warfield." Dayton, however, failed to mention that the person who was responsible for the school's present course was Harold John Ockenga. If Ockenga was a closet Methodist, how does one account for the present state of Gordon-Conwell?[65]

Marsden does not feel that doing a revisionist history from a holiness paradigm will assist in understanding the complexities of evangelical history. Douglas Sweeney agreed. In his article, Sweeney conceded that Dayton had a legitimate concern but Sweeney felt that Dayton built his argument out of questionable material. Sweeney did not agree with Dayton's assessment that true evangelicals oppose strict doctrinal orthodoxy. Sweeney believed Dayton's argument rested on the false assumption that Old School Calvinism and social conservatism set the standard of orthodoxy in the nineteenth-century. Sweeney believed this argument was complicated by Dayton's dependence on Charles Finney as the best representative of the "unorthodox" or "anti-orthodox" position. Sweeney felt this was a problem because, "Finney's apostasy only makes sense from within the 'Presbyterian' framework Dayton is opposing."[66] This problem is further complicated by the fact that high Calvinism and the Reformed tradition were not synonymous in the nineteenth-century. In the nineteenth-century high Calvinists lost control of the Reformed tradition. Sweeney argued that if orthodoxy was conceived in terms of power and influence, then high Calvinists like those at Princeton in the nineteenth-century were heterodox not orthodox. If this is true then where does Finney fit in Dayton's scheme?[67]

Joel Carpenter did not think Dayton's approach to the problem of evangelical historiography was a productive one. Carpenter believed that Dayton's true opponents were not neoevangelical historians but rather neoevangelical theologians: John Gerstner, Harold Lindsell, Bernard Ramm and Harold Ockenga. Dayton's argument, according to Carpenter, was that Marsden was influenced by these neoevangelical theologians. Carpenter countered Dayton's argument by suggesting that, in *Reforming Fundamentalism*, Marsden revealed the myths that neoevangelicals made of their heritage, and, in doing so, he revealed that the myth-makers were the theologians of that generation. Carpenter contended that if blame were placed anywhere for so much "Reformed historiography," it should be placed at the feet of intellectual history. Intellectual historians look for the ideas that motivate people and that is why Marsden and other historians tended to find the Calvinists tradition so intriguing. He argued that if the influences that shaped these Reformed historians were traced, you would find Perry Miller and Sydney Ahlstrom, not John Gerstner or Bernard Ramm.[68]

Is it possible to sort through this difficult dilemma of evangelical history? There is reason to believe that it is possible but the answer may lie within the problem. Nathan Hatch has recently devoted a considerable amount of time to the study of Methodism. He believes that American Methodism is the most understudied area of Protestant American religion. His Bartlett Address at Yale examined "The Puzzle of American Methodism."[69] He chides a generation of historians for either ignoring the value of Methodist studies or for sanitizing them to make Methodism seem more respectable to those enthralled by intellectual history.

Delivering the O. C. and Grace Tanner Lecture to Mormon historians he used the subject of American Methodism in comparing it to Mormon history. Hatch feels that early American Methodism offers the best insight into the nature of Christianity in America precisely because it was not respectable and status quo, but rather experimental, radical, and pragmatic. Hatch's description of Methodism and his appreciation for its contribution is reminiscent of Dayton's argument for Methodism as a grassroots movement. Finally, there is *Voices From the Heart: Four Centuries of American Piety*, a book co-authored by Mark Noll and Roger Lundin. In terms of history and theology, this book cuts across denominational lines to offer a look at piety as it found expression in a variety of traditions.[70]

These Reformed evangelical historians clearly do not speak for all evangelicals. They have offered their historical critiques and research to the evangelical community and that community has responded with mixed reviews. Though, like Schaeffer, these historians at times seem to identify being Christian with being evangelical when speaking of Christians in the early American republic, they disagree with Schaeffer on the actual influence those early Christians had on the political founding and direction of the nation. They do, however, seem to share with Schaeffer an interest in finding the evangelical influences in the early history of America, and they appear to draw their lines on who the Christians were a bit more narrowly than others might. Donald Dayton would say that they have narrowed their history to exclude all but those who are evangelical Calvinists. Dayton's argument may be a bit extreme but it does point out an area of weakness in these Reformed historians' research.

Notes

1. *The Times* (London) November 5, 1988.
2. Ibid.
3. Charles Lippy and Peter W. Williams, eds. *Encyclopedia of the American Religious Experience* (New York: Charles Scribner's Sons, 1988), s. v. "Conservative and Charismatic Developments of the Twentieth Century" by Richard Quebedeaux.
4. George M. Marsden, *Understanding Fundamentalism and Evangelicalism* (Grand Rapids: Wm. B. Eerdmans, 1991), 53-66.
5. George M. Marsden, *Reforming Fundamentalism: Fuller Seminary and the New Evangelicalism* (Grand Rapids: Wm. B. Eerdmans, 1987), 41-44.
6. Ibid., 103-111.
7. Ibid., 189.
8. Nathan Hatch Interview #2, June 3, 1993, University of Notre Dame.
9. Ibid.
10. Ibid.
11. Ibid.
12. Kenneth L. Woodward, "Guru of Fundamentalism," *Newsweek*, 1 November 1982, 88.
13. Marsden Interview, June 3, 1993, University of Notre Dame.
14. *The Spectacle* (Calvin College), vol. 1, no. 5, November 1, 1968.
15. Ibid.
16. Marsden Interview, June 3, 1993, University of Notre Dame.
17. George Marsden to Francis Schaeffer, February 15, 1982.
18. Ibid.
19. Ibid.
20. Francis Schaeffer to George Marsden, April 21, 1982.
21. Ibid.
22. Mark Noll to Francis Schaeffer, November 3, 1982.
23. Ibid. (Addendum attached to November 3 letter).
24. Mark Noll, "The Bible in Revolutionary America," a paper written in 1982 and provided to the author by Mark Noll along with additional correspondence, June 4, 1994.
25. Francis Schaeffer to Mark Noll, November 20, 1982.
26. Mark Noll to Francis Schaeffer, December 8, 1982.
27. Ibid.
28. Ibid.
29. Ibid.
30. Francis Schaeffer to Mark Noll, December 20, 1982.
31. George Marsden to Francis Schaeffer, January 13, 1983.
32. Ibid., Marsden commented further on the uses of history in his essay, "Evangelicals, History, and Modernity" in *Evangelicalism and Modern America* (Grand Rapids: Wm. B. Eerdmans Publishing, 1984), which he edited. In this essay he discussed how religious groups often used history to

establish a religious-national identity. They also used history to collect precedents from the past to support views they sought to defend in the present without regard to the flow of cultural history around them.

[33] Ibid.

[34] Mark Noll to Francis Schaeffer, January 13, 1983.

[35] Ibid.

[36] G. Aiken Taylor, "Francis Schaeffer: America's Historical Underpinnings" *The Presbyterian Journal* (March 2, 1983): 7, 8, & 13.

[37] George Marsden, "America's Origins Were Mixed" *The Presbyterian Journal* (March 30, 1983): 2.

[38] Henry F. Lazenby, "More About Witherspoon" *The Presbyterian Journal* (March 30, 1983): 2.

[39] Francis Schaeffer to Mark Noll, March 11, 1983.

[40] Francis A. Schaeffer, *The Great Evangelical Disaster* (Westchester: Crossway Books, 1984), 117-18.

[41] Ibid., 119.

[42] George Marsden to Francis Schaeffer, May 7, 1983.

[43] Mark Noll, Nathan Hatch, and George Marsden, *The Search for Christian America* (Westchester: Crossway Books, 1983), 16-17.

[44] Ibid., 129-140. There were lengthy end notes for this chapter which further expounded upon the nature of the historical arguments which Marsden sought to refute.

[45] Ibid., 148-55.

[46] See Randall Balmer, *Mine Eyes Have Seen the Glory: A Journey into the Evangelical Subculture in America* (New York: Oxford University Press, 1989) and Nathan O. Hatch, *The Democratization of American Christianity* (New Haven: Yale University Press, 1989).

[47] Donald W. Dayton, "Yet Another Layer of the Onion or Opening the Ecumenical Door and Let the Riffraff in" *The Ecumenical Review* 40, no. 1 (January 1988): 89-95.

[48] Ibid., 100.

[49] Ibid., 101.

[50] Donald Dayton, "Some Doubts about the Usefulness of the Category Evangelical" in *The Variety of American Evangelicalism*, eds. Donald W. Dayton and Robert K. Johnston (Downers Grove: InterVarsity Press, 1991), 247-51.

[51] Donald Dayton, "Reply to George Marsden" *Christian Scholar's Review* 7, no. 2,3 (1977): 207-10.

[52] Donald Dayton, in 1988 Preface to, *Discovering an Evangelical Heritage* (Peabody: Hendrickson Publishers, 1976), ix-xiii.

[53] Ibid., 120-35.

[54] Ibid., 138-41.

[55] George Marsden, "Demythologizing Evangelicalism: A Review of Donald Dayton's Discovering an Evangelical Heritage" *Christian Scholar's Review*

7, 2,3 (1977): 204-06. David Wells, in his paper "On Being Evangelical" delivered at a conference on Transatlantic Evangelicalism, April 8-11 1992 at Wheaton College, stated that he saw evangelicalism as a post WWII phenomenon. He reasoned that, "locating the spiritual forebears of today's evangelicals, and in finding theological antecedents upon which today's evangelicals can plant their feet will not shed light on how the contemporary evangelical world is thinking about its own theological nature."

[56] Douglas A. Sweeney, "The Essential Evangelical Dialectic: The Historiography of the Early Neoevangelical Movement and the Observer-Participant Dilemma" *Church History* 60 (March 1991): 70-84.

[57] George Marsden Interview, June 3, 1993, University of Notre Dame.

[58] Donald W. Dayton, "Rejoinder to Historiography Discussion" *Christian Scholar's Review* 23 (September 1993): 62.

[59] Donald W. Dayton, "'The Search for the Historical Evangelicalism: George Marsden's History of Fuller Seminary as a Case Study" *Christian Scholar's Review* 23 (September 1993): 14-27.

[60] Ibid., 18-19.

[61] Ibid., 20-21.

[62] George Marsden, "Response to Don Dayton" *Christian Scholar's Review* 23 (September 1993): 34-35.

[63] Ibid., 38.

[64] Ibid.

[65] Ibid., 39.

[66] Douglas A. Sweeney, "Historiographical Dialectics: On Marsden, Dayton, and the Inner Logic of Evangelical History" *Christian Scholar's Review* 23 (September 1993): 50.

[67] Ibid.

[68] Joel A. Carpenter, "The Scope of American Evangelicalism: Some Comments on the Dayton-Marsden Exchange" *Christian Scholar's Review* 23 (September 1993): 54-55, 60.

[69] Nathan O. Hatch, "The Puzzle of American Methodism," Delivered as the Bartlett Lecture, Yale University, February 9, 1993.

[70] Roger Lundin and Mark A. Noll, eds. *Voices From the Heart: Four Centuries of American Piety* (Grand Rapids: Wm. B. Eerdmans Publishing Company, 1987). In his review of this book, Charles Hambrick-Stowe found its focus to be too narrow when compared to its title. He applauded its ecumenicity but criticized it for missing the wider range of non-Christian spirituality. He wondered at the poor representation of the Black experience, the absence of a Greek or Russian Orthodox example, the over abundance of New England's contributions, and the small percentage of women. This review seems to indicate that neither the Holiness nor the Reformed traditions represent America's marginal groups. Charles Hambrick-Stowe, review of *Voices From the Heart: Four Centuries of American Piety* Roger Lundin and Mark A. Noll, eds., In *Church History* 57 (December 1988): 580.

4

The Opening of the Evangelical Mind

Mark Noll, Nathan Hatch, and George Marsden all express concern over the present state of higher education. They voice their concerns in two ways. First, they are disturbed by what they perceive as a lack of serious attention and money given by evangelicals to the advancement of scholarship among their institutions. Second, they believe that a Christian worldview is still a viable intellectual alternative in the university. In this respect, they are all part of an ongoing discussion among Christian institutions, Protestant and Catholic, who are asking if it is possible to provide a uniquely Christian education while simultaneously assuring academic freedom and a pluralistic faculty and student body. If it is possible to provide such an education, what would the structure of such an institution look like, how would it relate to the wider intellectual community, and how would this institution maintain a pluralistic student and faculty body without losing its Christian distinctiveness?

Once again the interplay between faith and learning poses a dilemma for these historians. They choose to move beyond the boundaries of their own discipline to address the wider philosophical question surrounding undergraduate and graduate education. They are interested in who sets the university's intellectual agenda because they believe whoever shapes the university's agenda ultimately shapes the cultural milieu.

Marsden, Hatch, and Noll are heirs of those neoevangelicals in the 40s and 50s who, through the pursuit of scholarship, thought they could "remake the modern mind." But these evangelical scions are more realistic in their assessment of the problems they face in the intellectually pluralistic world of academics. They realize that they represent only a part of that world and so must move carefully and purposefully if they hope to gain influence as scholars. Gaining influence means doing their homework and producing a high quality of scholarship in order to achieve what may be only begrudging respect from others, but respect nonetheless. They speak openly of their views on education and scholarship, utilizing the platforms and opportunities that their success affords them, but the measure of influence they have gained remains a matter for speculation.

The first part of this chapter will examine their views on both evangelical scholarship and their dialogue with those who face the challenges and complexities of providing a distinctly Christian education. These historians recognize that it is not appropriate to speak of evangelical scholarship and Christian scholarship as though they were synonymous. They acknowledge there are distinctions in the interests, agendas, and goals that separate specifically evangelical scholarship from broader Christian scholarship, but they believe that a Christian worldview provides a coherent educational philosophy for scholarship. Thus these evangelical historians are interested in establishing a broader base for scholarship than what an evangelical perspective alone could provide. This chapter explores the pertinent essays, addresses, and books written with the express purpose of reasserting a Christian tradition of scholarship for use by Christian educators in this century and the next.

The second part of this chapter traces the history of an organization which, conceived in a marriage between historical interests and personal friendships, has come to reflect and inculcate the intellectual aspirations and Christian commitments these historians bring to their scholarship. This organization has also become a centerpiece for an ongoing controversy between these historians and other evangelicals over the proper place and function of scholarship.

Christian Scholarship?

The interests these men have in Christian education could be described as three interlocking pieces of a jigsaw puzzle. Each piece has its own distinctive shape and color but the shape and color only make sense when the three pieces are united to form the whole puzzle. In addition, each piece of the puzzle raises an important question which must be answered if the pieces are to fit. One of the pieces represents the place and contribution of evangelical scholarship to the larger enterprise of Christian learning. This piece of the puzzle will be examined in a separate section. The purpose of this section on Christian scholarship is to examine the other two pieces.

The first piece of the puzzle represents the shape and color of the modern American university. This part of the puzzle raises the question of how the modern American university received its shape. Was this its original shape, and, if this is not its original shape, what cultural and educational forces contributed to its metamorphoses?

The second piece of the puzzle represents the shape and color of Christian education. This piece poses the question of whether a Christian worldview provides a coherent educational philosophy for an academic marketplace that is currently seeking a common foundation for its many disciplines? If a Christian worldview does provide that foundation, what problems does this raise for Christian educators trying to work within the present academic guidelines designed to operate in the pluralistic environment of a modern secular university?

The Shape of the Modern University

George Marsden has devoted much time and energy researching the first of these pieces of the puzzle. He has written articles, essays, and two books on the shape and philosophy of the modern American university. The titles of his two books, the first of which he co-edited with Bradley Longfield, are indicative of his thesis that the modern American university is the product of a process of theological and cultural secularization. These two books are, *The Secularization of the Academy* and *The Soul of the American University: From Protestant Establishment to Established Non-Belief.*

Marsden uses the process of secularization to describe the way in which the American university's educational philosophy changed in its relationship to the Christian educational philosophy that once undergirded it. He believes the nature of that change between the modern university's educational philosophy and that of its earlier Christian philosophy of education was one of moving from "the same as" to "in common with" until finally it became "opposed to."[1] Although he believes that the change in this role of religion in higher education has resulted in a loss, he does not associate the process of secularization with a decline in education per se, nor does he want to see the control of public education returned to a religious establishment.[2] In other words, he rejects the idea that there is a golden age of Christian education that needs to be recaptured.

Instead, Marsden reexamines the early history of American higher education, taking into account the strong Protestant religious heritage that provided a foundation for many of the modern premier universities. He hopes that this reexamination will answer the questions of why and how the university changed so drastically within the last century? Speaking of the need for this kind of historical review Marsden wrote, "That many educated people today are unaware that until so recently leading American schools promoted Christianity is one index of how secular the current scene has become. Winners get to write the histories first, so the histories of higher education generally have been as secular as the academy itself."

By raising questions about the history of the modern American university, Marsden is able to challenge the undergirding presuppositions of the modern academy, particularly the idea of "academic freedom." Marsden argues that the concepts of value-free academic inquiry and the promotion of individual freedom are based largely on a myth generated by the Enlightenment. Nicholas Wolterstorff and Alvin Plantinga present similar views in *Faith and Rationality: Reason and Belief in God*.[3] Alasdair MacIntyre, in his book *Three Rival Versions of Moral Enquiry: Encyclopaedia, Genealogy, and Tradition*,[4] also questions the possibility of objective or "value-free" scholarship based on an Enlightenment paradigm. Marsden follows this same line of thought when he contends that the Enlightenment idea of objective value-free science is used to discredit a Christian philosophy of education. But since this idea has recently been routed in some academic circles, Marsden concludes that the academy should reexamine the basis upon which he believes it relegated a Christian worldview to a marginal position in the university.[5]

Marsden examines three forces that shaped the modern American university and explains why Protestants, who used to control the university system, have "forsaken it so recently and forgotten it so completely," and why Christianity came to be considered a hindrance to academic progress and expression.[6] The three forces he examines are: the demands of a post Civil War technological society, conflicts over ideology, and the complexities of an increasingly pluralistic society.

Marsden argues that, before and just after the Civil War, college education in America was taught by clerics and was based on the Western model of expertise in the classics. The central element in this classical curriculum was a course in Moral Philosophy usually taught by the president of the school who was often a cleric. With the end of the Civil War, American society entered a time of technological advancement which precipitated two changes in the university system. The government encouraged schools to design their curriculums around technology and agriculture, and assisted these changes with monetary incentives. The other change involved a move toward more specialization in graduate research designed to produce more scholars in specialty areas. This change was deemed necessary because the former curriculum built around the classics did not produce a high degree of specialized scholarship.[7]

Marsden indicates that these changes in turn produced a gradual shift in attitude toward classical education. The traditional method of education taught by clerics was now seen as old fashioned and amateurish by proponents of the newer educational trends. The clerically operated schools resisted this intrusion of technological and specialized studies and were therefore labeled opponents of educational openness and scientific advancement. This labeling was taken one step further by educational reformers who determined that if higher education was to achieve status as a separate profession, it must first be freed from clerical control and, subsequently, from traditional Christianity.[8]

Thus, the prevailing winds of public education shifted in the late nineteenth and early twentieth-centuries forcing a change in direction for the Protestant based American educational system. Marsden finds great significance in the fact that the founders of many of the new universities in America around this time were liberal Protestants. These Protestants tended to follow a form of postmillennialism that emphasized the progress of humanity through scientific and technological means. The betterment of mankind was based upon this optimistic vision of reaching moral ends through scientific means. These liberal Protestants believed that this vision was consistent with Christian teaching concerning the advent of God's kingdom on earth. In pursuing this vision they helped move the change in educational philosophy from being "the same as" a Christian philosophy of education to being "in common with" that philosophy.

Marsden says that in the process they also helped to speed up the process of methodological secularization. By methodological secularization, Marsden means the generally accepted idea that for science to pursue its goals freely it must be liberated from dogma. To be liberated from dogma, science must be freed from the churches and from Christianity. The final outcome of this process was the belief that obtaining scientific objectivity for specialized research required the suspension of religious belief. It was only a short step from this view to one that advanced the notion that academic freedom necessitated the suspension and even removal of religious belief.[9]

The second force Marsden examines is ideological conflict and its consequences. Marsden contends that Christians assured the eventual victory of secular thought in the university system by assisting thoroughgoing secularism in its conflict with traditional Christianity. Liberal Protestants joined forces with the followers of Comtean positivism to promote a brand of moral values based upon the tenets of the Western humanities rather Christian principles. Pragmatism ruled the day. The dignity of man became the new phrase promoted by the humanities and around which a public consensus on values was built. "Since public consensus was the ideal, however, it was best to be low-key, entirely civil, and inclusive about one's faith. Although explicit Christians could play supporting or even mildly dissenting roles (Reinhold Niebuhr comes to mind), the essential ideals of society that higher education would promote were defined in secular terms and largely by secularists or by Christians who in academic settings thought they must speak as secularists."[10]

The final force Marsden holds responsible for the present shape of the university is cultural pluralism. He paints a picture of a dominant Protestant culture in control of higher education in the nineteenth-century but embarrassed over its exclusive religious claims. While society became increasingly pluralistic, the Protestant establishment continued to promote views that risked alienating a segment of that population. While they claimed to assent to the new cultural values of openness and objectivity, they appeared to promote exclusive beliefs. As a result, the Protestant establishment were faced with the dilemma of whether they could help shape the culture while maintaining distinctive Christian features?

The answer for many Protestant schools was to abandon their distinctively Christian features in favor of a more acceptable and broadly American value system that was based on democracy and moral character. The pressure on religious institutions from the academic community was directed toward the desire to create a healthy diversity among all institutions. Marsden contends that the end result was a kind of forced uniformity that required religious institutions to give up their distinctiveness under the threat of either losing their accreditation or being labeled as second class institutions. Features like compulsory chapel and required religion courses were eventually made voluntary with the result that "religious activity had moved from the center to the voluntary periphery."[11] Distinctive Christian ideals were exchanged for vague notions of democracy and civic humanity. This exchange was made with the hope that the scientific method would provide objective moral principles around which all of humanity could be united.[12]

Marsden argues that the cumulative results of these forces on higher education moved religion, and evangelical Christianity specifically, from the center of the university to the margins. When the sixties revolution in American society flowed over into the university, the full secularization of the educational system was complete. By the end of this decade even Christianity's role in helping to define the moral course of the university was removed and relegated to a position among the social sciences.[13]

Marsden's thesis suggests that the baby was thrown out with the bath water. He does not advocate a reestablishment of the Protestant hegemony in higher education, nor does he decry all the effects of secularization. He acknowledges the benefits to research that have been derived from the modern university system, benefits that have assisted him in his own research projects. But he does believe that the shapers of the modern university make an unsubstantiated assumption when they reject Christianity as a valid intellectual position. Marsden believes this rejection is unsubstantiated because the modern university bases its rejection of Christianity upon what Marsden considers to be outmoded concepts of scientific objectivity and value-free research. He believes the concept of "academic freedom" has become an educational dogma in the university that rivals the concern early educators had for religious dogma. Rather than promoting intellectual freedom, Marsden contends that this concept perpetuates a prejudice which is now more difficult to defend because of its questionable philosophical underpinnings. He believes that Christianity still represents an academically viable position even after the collapse of the Protestant educational establishment.

The Myth of "Academic Freedom"

The second piece of the puzzle represents the challenges faced by Christian education. The first of these challenges was the concept of "academic freedom." In his review of Jaroslav Pelikan's book, *The Idea of the University: A Reexamination*, Marsden challenges Pelikan's idea of the "multiversity," calling it an oxymoron.[14] He disagrees with Pelikan's assessment that the modern university is fulfilling the moral purpose of serving humanity. Marsden's argument is that the modern university's acceptance of purely naturalistic standards has left it without a single unified intellectual basis for pursuing the moral goals to which they aspire. The result is a morass of political debates among its many diverse disciplines reminiscent of Sydney Mead's remark that the modern university is actually a group of autonomous disciplines connected only by a central heating system.

The problem of the university having no unified intellectual tradition is, in Marsden's thinking, a symptom of a broader intellectual vacuum created by the recent demise of the Enlightenment principle of objective, value-free, scientific research. The Enlightenment principle of objective science was once touted by the academic world as a universally valid rationality. It was thought by the early founders of the modern university that in order to achieve this new scientific rationality the educational process must first be stripped of any traditional dogma, or sources of authority founded on revelation. But now, Marsden says, "the Enlightenment is over."[15]

Based upon this development, Marsden makes the following observations:

It is far less recognized that as the Enlightenment ideal has dissipated, so have the intellectual reasons for the a priori exclusion of theologically informed perspectives. There is no reason why an intellectually pluralist environment should not allow room for intellectually rigorous, theologically informed perspectives to compete on equal grounds with other perspectives. . . . Finally, the intellectual and cultural revolutions of recent decades should revise conventional wisdom regarding church related institutions. Throughout much of this century such institutions, to the extent that they were discernibly Christian, were regarded as unscientific and unprofessional. With the demise of Enlightenment ideals about universal science and objectivity, the intellectual reasons for such dogmatic attitudes have collapsed. Those who wish to relate their theological beliefs to the rest of their intellectual life have nothing to apologize for intellectually.[16]

Marsden associates the dogmatic attitudes in this quote with the professional guidelines established by the American Association of University Professors (AAUP). In his Presidential address to the American Society of Church History (ASCH) entitled, "The Ambiguities of Academic Freedom," Marsden used his research on the evolution of the phrase "academic freedom" to build a case for readmitting Christianity as a viable intellectual view in the university. He examined how the AAUP gradually built a wall of credibility between those institutions that maintained religious distinctions and those that did not. He researched an academic conflict at Lafayette College in the early twentieth-century as a test case to show how the AAUP used this conflict to build precedence for further cases involving religious institutions.

Marsden quoted from the report issued by the AAUP at its annual meeting in 1915. This report followed the findings of the AAUP regarding the Lafayette case which stated that American colleges and universities were essentially of two different types. Schools that were affiliated with denominations or had other religious ties were instruments of propaganda while schools without religious ties were true centers of academic freedom. The AAUP was especially concerned that these religious institutions not be allowed to present themselves as having the same academic credibility as those not affiliated with religion.[17]

Marsden pointed out that early on the idea of "academic freedom" was closely associated with the more ambiguous concept of "the common good." As time went by it was "the common good" and not "academic freedom" that became the academic absolute. The problem was that an idea like "the common good" became victim to the subjective interpretation of whoever was in charge of the university system. The "common good" usually meant the values reflected by the "white male Anglo establishment that had always run the university."[18]

Whether the phrase was "academic freedom" or "the common good," Marsden argued that neither could be defended any longer as an intellectual barrier to the expression of religious views because of the collapse of the Enlightenment principles that undergirded them. The failure of scientific inquiry to produce a universal rationality should, in Marsden's estimation, require a reexamination of the academy's opposition to the intellectual viability of religious views. He called any continuation of this opposition a matter of "sheer prejudice."[19]

Marsden concluded his remarks with this challenge to the ASCH:

> It is fair to say, however, that for several generations the prevailing style expected in the ASCH has been to hide the relationship of one's faith to one's scholarship. Even those who have been most ardent in their religious beliefs usually have been eager to demonstrate that they are just as professional and scientifically detached as other historians. Those who have been religiously committed, then, have in effect accepted ideals of scientific objectivity and detachment that became normative at the beginning of this century. Like the religious colleges who abandoned the task of relating Christianity to learning when they were told that was a second-class enterprise, so many historians of Christianity have acted as though they believed that relating their faith to their history would disqualify them from professional acceptability. At the end of the twentieth-century, however, we may be approaching a new era of openness to explicit academic commitment.[20]

Marsden raises an interesting question when he asks whether the American university should reconsider its decision to marginalize a Christian worldview as an equally valid intellectual alternative. If one accepts, as Marsden seems to, the postmodern premise that because the Enlightenment's preoccupation with objectivity failed to assess honestly the influence of subjective factors such as culture, and personal bias, therefore the Enlightenment's intellectual authority no longer holds a mandate in the university, then it would appear that Marsden's argument for rejecting the Enlightenment has validity. But Marsden does not promote postmodern thought as a valid philosophy for the university. He promotes Christianity. He does not appear to offer Christianity as the heir apparent to the Enlightenment, but if the Enlightenment can no longer provide a unified intellectual tradition for the university, then there is a problem.

Reason as a universal principle was the basis for the Enlightenment tradition. Reason allowed for all intellectual options but it favored some over others. Those traditions with a basis of authority in revelation were not considered a reliable source of authority when compared to those claiming reason alone. Revelation was not reliable as a basis of authority because it did not meet the Enlightenment criteria for objective science. The Enlightenment idea of reason provided a unified intellectual tradition that was pluralistic but biased. If that tradition is now passe, what is the alternative?

The relativism of postmodernist thought does not provide a unified tradition but it does create a rich pluralistic environment. If Marsden says that the Enlightenment is over then what will take its place? He finds value in the Enlightenment's demise because he feels that this will allow a Christian worldview more freedom to operate, but if the Enlightenment base is indeed gone there seems to be a vacuum. What if relativism fills that vacuum? Would Marsden rather have a Christian worldview compete in a relativistic atmosphere of no consensus or an Enlightenment atmosphere of unity with diversity? The university is a place where pluralism exists as a part of learning. If Marsden believes that Christianity could provide a unified tradition to replace the Enlightenment and offer a substitute for postmodern thought, how would pluralism be maintained in the faculty? This dilemma of promoting a Christian intellectual tradition that allows for true pluralism is faced by many sectarian universities, and poses a potential dilemma for Marsden as well.

The Challenge to and Response of Christian Institutions

In August of 1992, Nathan Hatch delivered the H. I. Hester Lecture during the National Conference on Integrating Personal Faith and Professional Discipline at Samford University. His lecture was entitled, "Christian Thinking in a Time of Academic Turmoil." He prefaced his talk by saying that as a Christian and as a professional academic, no issue could be more pressing than the immediate attempts being made to integrate Christian faith and academic life. He built the content of his talk around three challenges that faced any who sought to balance serious intellectual pursuits with commitments to Christian values.[21]

The first challenge involved the erosion of public trust in higher education. Hatch reflected upon the long history of university education stretching back through the centuries. The university had once been considered a place for reform and vision. It was once respected for its efforts to help give society a sense of direction. Now, due to increasing costs, charges of abuse of power among faculty and staff, and controversies over political correctness, the university seemed to have become a center of greed and elitism. There was now a serious question of whether the university could any longer communicate a message of trust and help to the public at large. Hatch saw this erosion of public trust as an opportunity as well as a problem. It was an opportunity for those who took the challenge of forming new alliances, gathering fresh vision, and seeking stronger leadership to make a new beginning.

The divorce between piety and learning represented a second challenge. Hatch bemoaned the fact that the church's growth in the West over the last century appeared to be directly proportional to the failure of Christianity as a intellectual force in Western society. Hatch agreed with Marsden's assessment of the power and influence secularization enjoyed in higher education, but Hatch added a second influence, that of religious populism. The power of populism as a driving force in American Christianity is a common theme explored by Hatch in his book, *The Democratization of American Christianity*. Populism, in Hatch's interpretation, represented the joining of various forms of Christian polity with the democratic orientation of the American republic. Those forms of Christianity that prospered in America were characterized by their ability to gain and maintain popular support. Thus, as a result, a gulf existed between the educated elite in secular American culture and the world of popular Christianity where the focus was on "breadth of audience rather than depth of insight."[22]

Religious populism raised various problems for leaders in Christian education. The main problem was that issues of great complexities tended to be flattened out for popular consumption with the result that the lines between clarification and falsification were often blurred. For example, the issue of inerrancy, when discussed among Southern Baptists, often degenerates into a war of words and accusations. The result is that often the theological and historical complexities of the issue are either reduced to the simplistic rhetoric of whether someone really believed the Bible or becomes subservient to the personalities arguing the issue. In either scenario, the relevant and complex facts of the issue are lost in the attempts, by both sides, to rally popular support. Another related problem involved the impressions such problem solving techniques gave the secular intellectual world. These impressions included: reinforcement of the opinion that Christians had nothing to say that would be intellectually coherent or compelling, placing Christian scholars in the untenable position of trying to find creative and lasting solutions without transgressing boundaries established by the popular courts that employed them, and finally, these techniques threatened to hasten the process of secularization in Christian education when Christian institutions gave up their distinctiveness in order to escape the threat of fundamentalist control.[23]

The final challenge Hatch discussed was the crisis of authority in the modern university. To illustrate this crisis of authority, Hatch examined the crisis as reflected in several disciplines. In literary criticism he pointed out the growing influence of a deconstructionist school of thought. This school represented the intention to fragment either the objective meaning in any text and reduce it to separate disconnected shards, or to find meaning in the reader alone. In other words this school represented a strict brand of relativism. Once one moved from literary questions to moral ones then it was clear that there was no consensus.

In legal studies Hatch referred to what he called "situational jurisprudence." The lack of continuity in legal decisions, particularly in Supreme Court decisions, created a school of legal thought that viewed law as a mere extension of the political process. In other words, law reflected the prevailing tone of the day. The common element in both of these examples was the adoption of relativism as a postmodernist source of authority in place of the former Enlightenment principle of objective scientific authority.[24]

In response to these challenges Hatch offered three suggestions to Christian educators. These three suggestions all presupposed that the greatest task of Christian educators was to train, attract, and develop a strong faculty that understood the challenges it faced in providing a Christian education. His first suggestion was to make sure that department heads who influenced the selection of professors embodied the highest ideals of the university. This was crucial at a time when many forces in academic departments tended to pull away from the center resulting in a lack of unity in purpose and thought. Second, he felt there must be more intentional engagement in the process of selecting faculty, something more than posting the position, selecting a few people to interview, and then hiring someone. Someone should know who the best teachers were in that discipline, teachers who were also committed to Christian values. Character and commitment should matter as much as credentials. Finally, he encouraged them not to specialize themselves out of the best candidates for the position. If character, belief, and faith were important then educators should be flexible in adapting guidelines to get the best people. In order to accomplish this goal they might be wise to go beyond the walls of their own religious community.

Before proceeding into the next section on evangelical scholarship it is important to remember that both Marsden and Hatch are professors at the University of Notre Dame. Marsden holds the McAnaney Professorship in History, while Hatch is a professor in the history department in addition to being the Vice President for Graduate Studies and Research. These two Reformed evangelicals found a home at the premier Catholic University in America, and they are not alone.[25] Alvin Plantinga is director of Notre Dame's Center for Philosophy of Religion and John Van Engen is the Conway Director of the Medieval Institute. So why are Reformed evangelical Protestants holding significant academic and administrative positions at Notre Dame?

George Marsden attributes this phenomenon to Notre Dame's commitment and openness to scholarship. This openness has allowed a significant group of people interested in asking questions about the relationship between Christianity and scholarship to gather and pursue these questions. Marsden thinks it is significant that the great majority of these Reformed scholars are part of the Dutch Reformed tradition that takes the life of the mind seriously. He believes the Dutch Reformed tradition largely parallels that of the Neo-Thomist tradition in Catholicism.[26]

The Dutch Reformed position in America, alluded to by Marsden, was heavily indebted to the thinking of Abraham Kuyper. Kuyper held to what could be called a Calvinistic Weltanschauung.[27] This worldview classified the human race into two groups, the Normalist and Abnormalist. Each held a different scientific viewpoint. The Normalist held a naturalistic viewpoint which declared God unknowable and the bulk of Christian doctrine as impossible. The Abnormalist was essentially Augustinian in outlook. God was creator and humans were made in his image. Sin was all pervasive and corrupting and therefore only an act of God could restore humanity. The result of these differences were that even though these two types of people saw the same facts, they interpreted the facts from two different sets of presuppositions.[28]

Marsden is committed to working in a community where both the church and society are served, but where primary loyalty is reserved for Christian values when the two are in conflict. He is committed to steering, if possible, a middle ground between excellence in scholarship and maintaining Christian distinctives. He is impressed by the number of Christians who do not think Christian scholarship matters, and thinks a book may be needed on what it means to be a Christian scholar.[29]

Hatch prefers to think in terms of Christian scholars finding a home at Notre Dame rather than evangelical scholars. He does not think there is very much evangelical scholarship being done but he believes there is a significant amount of Christian scholarship. He attributes the lack of evangelical scholarship to the absence of a strong intellectual tradition among evangelicals as a whole with the exception of the Dutch Reformed faith. Hatch thinks the Dutch Reformed tradition of scholarship is similar to that of Roman Catholicism because they both draw upon the classical heritage of Christian education. Within these two groups Hatch believes one can find a scholarly heritage that draws upon the classical tradition of Christian education. "We take Christian scholarship seriously but not in a narrow way. There is some scholarship that will come out the same whether Christians or non-Christians do it. (This would seem to contradict Kuyper's view of two distinct sciences). It is trying to do academic work in light of certain principles without compromising the quality of academic work."[30]

Hatch believes that Notre Dame is in the unique position of being a university with firm religious roots with no intention of giving them up, but aspiring to be a first rate university. With these goals in mind he authored a booklet on Notre Dame's aspirations and achievements in promoting a high level of graduate education and research. In this booklet Hatch outlined Notre Dame's progress in becoming a premier research university. On the last page of this publication under a section called, "Cutting Against the Grain," Hatch makes the following remarks which echo his and Marsden's convictions about Christian scholarship:

> Notre Dame's experiment in building a university of sterling quality and revitalizing Catholic intellectual life is far from complete. To realize these dreams will require renewed commitment, enormous resources, and a willingness to hew an independent course. At a time of serious entrenchment in higher education, Notre Dame intends to press for continued enhancement of its academic programs. At a time when the aims of teaching and research seem discordant, Notre Dame intends to preserve them as complementary missions. And at a time of wide divorce between the academy and the church, Notre Dame intends to frame a university both authentically Catholic and accountable to the highest standards of scholarship.[31]

Evangelical Scholarship

Marsden wrote an article in the June 1988 issue of *The Christian Scholar's Review* called "The State of Evangelical Christian Scholarship." In this article he traced the recent history of evangelical scholarship from its loss of influence and credibility at the beginning of the twentieth-century to its attempt at recapturing that influence in the 1940s. In this article he raised the important question of whether interest in scholarship among evangelicals was actually creating the emergence of "an evangelical Christian Renaissance" or whether it was "simply introducing secular standards to its community?"[32]

He then digressed forty years earlier to discuss the heyday of evangelical scholarship led by men like Carl F. H. Henry and Harold John Ockenga and represented by the founding of Fuller Seminary. Marsden pointed out that not all those who were on the faculty at Fuller were scholars; in fact, the list of true scholars among evangelical ranks at this time was quite short. Henry and Ockenga hoped for a renewal of evangelical scholarship that would "remake the modern mind." They envisioned evangelical scholarship providing a challenge to the ruling presuppositions of the secular mind. Their methodology followed that of Abraham Kuyper and his concept of antithesis between the Christian mind and the secular mind. Kuyper's methodology emphasized the need to examine presuppositions carefully.[33] This early experiment in evangelical scholarship failed to reshape the modern mind as Henry and Ockenga had hoped. But it did provide a springboard for future evangelicals to take the life of the mind seriously.

Marsden then defined two counterforces at work in the evangelical community's attempt to gain academic credibility. The first counterforce was the failure of liberalism and, hopefully, the lesson learned from the modernist/fundamentalist debates. Marsden appealed for the need of intellectual maturity among evangelicals if they were to benefit from the lessons of their past and avoid being swept in either direction.

The triumph of Kuyperian presuppositionalism was the second counterforce. Marsden felt the Kuyperian method of defining a position's presuppositions had won the day against the common-sense Baconian thought that once ruled evangelicals. Baconian thought insisted that there was one objective science for all people and therefore "there should be no real distinction between Christian thinking and clear thinking."[34] Kuyperian thought emphasized a distinction between Christian and non-Christian thought that was the result of their being founded on opposing first principles.

Marsden outlined what he considered a basic agenda for evangelical scholarship:

> Helping to establish the intellectual viability of our worldview can
> be an important service to our community and an important

dimension of our witness to the world. To perform this task properly requires a delicate combination of modesty and assertiveness. Our intellectual life must display the Christian qualities of self-criticism and generosity to others. . . . Establishing the attractiveness of a worldview, however, is not strictly or even primarily an intellectual enterprise. Rather we should hope that evangelical Christians will demonstrate the attractiveness of our worldview by the way our communities address the whole range of human experience. This involves the way we live and not just the way we think. . . . This does not mean that action is identical with intellectual life or can be substituted for it.[35]

Mark Noll also did not think action was a substitute for intellectual life. Though he believed that evangelicals must act on their convictions, he felt they could not afford to abandon the life of intellectual reflection. When he gave the McManis Installation Lecture on "The Scandal of the Evangelical Mind" at Wheaton College in February of 1993 he noted:

So what if American evangelicals commit themselves much more thoroughly to creating TV networks than to creating universities? So what if evangelical activism allows scant room for cultivation of the mind? So what if evangelical populism regularly verges into anti-intellectualism? What—from the standpoint of essential Christian truth—is at stake in letting the mind go to waste?[36]

According to Noll everything that was valuable to a distinct Christian witness in American culture was at stake. He was concerned with evangelical scholarship as well as the cultivation of Christian thinking across the whole spectrum of life and learning. His emphasis on the cultivation of Christian thinking in every area of life, like Marsden's, showed a similar dependence on Dutch Calvinism.

For Noll, the bottom line was, who sets the agenda for the academy and, consequently, the culture at large? The universities with the money and the resources to promote research set the agenda. Those universities then became the "gatekeepers, intellectual and physical, for most of the learned professions. . . . Such universities also have a correspondingly greater influence on the world of scholarship."[37] Noll supported his argument by quoting from Charles Malik's speech given at Wheaton College in honor of the opening of the Billy Graham Center in 1980:

. . . at the heart of the crisis in Western civilization lies the state of the mind and the spirit of the universities. . . . The greatest danger besetting American Evangelical Christianity is the danger of anti-intellectualism. . . . Who among the evangelical scholars is quoted as a normative source by the greatest secular authorities on history or philosophy or psychology or sociology or politics? For the sake of greater effectiveness in witnessing to Jesus Christ Himself, as well as for their own sakes, the Evangelicals cannot afford to keep on living on the periphery of responsible intellectual existence.[38]

Noll became quite vehement in his appeal for fellow evangelicals to take seriously the need of developing a sharp incisive Christian mind. He referred to those evangelicals who were willing to concede to "the world" the intellectual operations of the university as being either gnostics, Manicheans, or docetists. In other words he considered them to be intellectual heretics.[39]

Noll closed his talk by asking three questions he felt summarized what was at stake for evangelicals. First, he asked who would be the tutors to teach present and future evangelicals and their children about life? Would the mass media or Madison Avenue be the teachers? His second question asked how evangelicals would live in the world. Noll encouraged his listeners to take seriously their daily living and receive it as a gift from God to be thought about carefully in the light of eternity. This question was reminiscent of Marsden's comment on the need for evangelicals to demonstrate the attractiveness of their worldview through their lifestyle as well as their thinking. The final question was, what kind of God will evangelicals worship? Noll emphasized that the God they worshiped was the one who created all things and revealed himself in Jesus Christ. He was therefore a God they could know. "From this perspective the search for a Christian mind takes on ultimate significance, because the search for a Christian mind is not, in the end, a search for mind, but a search for God."[40]

These historian's critiques are not the same as the assessment of American higher education offered by Allan Bloom. They do not attribute the loss of a basis of authority in the university to its abandonment of a liberal arts curriculum based on the classics.[41] They do not believe a reestablishment of the ideals of western civilization is the answer. They want to see room made in the university for a Christian worldview, but realize that this will not happen because they wish it to be so or believe that it would be more fair if it were. They believe the answer lies in the hands of Christian scholars in general and evangelical scholars specifically. These scholars must combine rigorous research with personal integrity to influence a change in the academy's attitude. They also think, on a more practical note, that in order to effect such a change, evangelicals must start putting their money where their mouth is. Toward this end, conferences and meetings have been held by evangelicals and other interested Christians to discuss the merits and obstacles of a Christian graduate school or a Christian university.

Nathan Hatch and George Marsden contributed to such a conference held at Messiah College in May of 1993. Marsden directed his remarks to the question of whether it was possible for Christianity to regain a voice in the university. Essentially, Marsden did not think such a venture would prove fruitful. He based this assessment on his study of the academy's evolution over the last century. Based on this research he concluded that the academy would not tolerate such an institution even if such an institution took the form of a "free-standing graduate college," "associated with a research university."[42] The academy would not tolerate such an institution because it would violate the present standards of academic freedom. In addition, if it failed to promote a democratic cultural ideal then its charter would fail the test of pluralism, which, for Marsden, was another word for uniformity.[43] Marsden did not despair entirely. He felt there was still hope for such a venture provided those who directed it were aware of and prepared for the obstacles.

Hatch also participated in this conference. He responded to a paper delivered by George Keller. The dilemma Hatch presented was the need for finding a working model of a Christian university. Had there ever been such a thing? He went on to say, that based upon his experience, he saw three major challenges to such an enterprise. The first challenge was overcoming evangelical suspicion of intellectual pursuits. Hatch did not believe that evangelicals had the kind of commitment to Christian thinking that was necessary to produce a great graduate school. Evangelicals tended to find their authority in the confines of their own courts of popular opinion, and were distrustful of intellectuals. He gave, as an example, the actions taken by the Billy Graham Center (BGC) to distance itself from the purpose and work of the Institute for the Study of American Evangelicals (ISAE) which was formerly a part of the BGC but was gradually pushed out. These actions were based to a significant degree on the BGC's discomfort with activities that appeared to be solely intellectual.[44] The relationship between these two entities will be discussed further in the next section of this chapter.

Hatch also pointed out the problem of boundaries. Evangelicals were known for establishing boundaries of all types to maintain their various distinctives. The problem with boundaries is heightened by the diversity among evangelicals. With such diversity, whose boundaries would be normative for a university funded and controlled by evangelicals? Whose views would set the pace? Moderate positions would be pressed from both sides with the effect that people who trespass boundaries would not be trusted. This problem alone makes the idea of an evangelical university untenable.[45]

Hatch then turned to the practical problem of resources. As Vice President of Graduate Studies and Research at Notre Dame, Hatch brought his experience on the cost graduate of education to the discussion. He felt that even a grant of $25 to $50 million was not sufficient to produce and maintain a superb graduate school. The cost of graduate fellowships and tuition scholarships alone would soon deplete such resources. In addition, he proposed that a competitive graduate faculty must be given a two-two teaching load, two courses per semester. The final practical question was where would those who received their degrees find employment? Because of the source of their degrees, they could be easily overlooked in the marketplace.[46]

Hatch offered an alternative strategy in the form of two suggestions. He encouraged Christian educators to strengthen their existing undergraduate programs. He felt this goal was the first and most crucial aspect if Christian colleges were to attract the best students. They must equip undergraduates with a model for integrating faith and learning and then send them to the best graduate schools prepared for engaging the intellectual world. He further suggested that graduate education needed to be supplemented with research foundations and institutes for use in networking students and faculty. Seminars and other opportunities were needed for students to interact with scholars who were asking vital and pressing contemporary questions. Hatch felt programs of this type were essential if Christian graduate students were to be prepared and inspired for future scholarship.[47]

The next section of this chapter will explore the practical steps taken by these historians to create just such an institution to supplement graduate work and allow an ongoing exchange of ideas among those interested in evangelical concerns. The ISAE offers a window through which one can observe the internal dynamics and influence of these historians as well as the problems they encounter when pursuing scholarship as evangelicals.

The Institute for the Study of American Evangelicals (ISAE)

The story of the ISAE actually begins with events described in the introduction to the first chapter of this study. It is a story of personal friendships, professional connections, and scholarly interests. The history of the ISAE is the story of how these various dynamics were combined over a period of five years to produce an organization that now networks historians, sociologists, and theologians from several countries for the purpose of exploring the issues and concerns of those diverse people who call themselves evangelicals. The ISAE is also a picture of evangelical scholars seeking to engage the wider academic world and how this attempt has fared among those in their own religious community. This section picks up the narrative begun in chapter one.

The informal meeting that occurred in a Deerfield, Illinois restaurant was significant because it set in motion a series of events that would eventually lead to the founding of the ISAE. The primary players in this unfolding story were Mark Noll, Nathan Hatch, and Robert Linn. Reflecting on this period Mark Noll said, "What was happening was a network was being built of people interested in the same things with an angle which was sympathetically Christian but was also critical of evangelicalism."[48]

At the conclusion of the Trinity conference in 1977, several of those who took part met for dinner at a local restaurant. The conversation eventually centered around a common concern over the way some evangelicals were using the Bible. The idea was suggested that there should be another conference on the historical use of the Bible. Nathan Hatch offered to check with Robert Linn at the Lilly Foundation to see if they would be interested in sponsoring such a conference.

Nathan Hatch approached Robert Linn with the idea of a conference on the historical use of the Bible,[49] and the Lilly Foundation provided $15,000.00 to fund the conference and a book comprised of the conference papers edited by Hatch and Noll.[50] The conference took place at Wheaton College in November of 1979 and was sponsored by the Lilly Foundation and Wheaton College.[51] The location for the conference was influenced by the addition of Mark Noll to the Wheaton History Department in the Fall of 1979. Noll found support for the conference among the Wheaton faculty and the administrators of the newly constructed Billy Graham Center who wanted to sponsor something academic.

But there was opposition from some who were uncomfortable with Wheaton sponsoring a conference that included academics such as Ernest Sandeen, who was known for being critical of evangelicalism. Noll attributed the conference's acceptance to the Wheaton trustees who bore the brunt of that opposition because they understood the difference between academic discussion and advocacy.[52] In addition to Sandeen, other participants included: Bruce Metzger, Richard Mouw, Timothy Smith, Harry Stout, Grant Wacker, George Marsden, Joel Carpenter, Donald Bloesch, Sydney Ahlstrom, E. Brooks Holifield, Timothy Weber, David Wells, and Kenneth Woodward.[53]

The details of who initially came up with the idea for the ISAE is sketchy, but around the time of this conference on the Bible there was already discussion and planning for a center dedicated to the study of American evangelicalism. Noll attributed the idea to Robert Linn, who, after attending the Wheaton conference, told Nathan Hatch that it was better than other conferences sponsored by the Lilly Foundation. Linn also observed that the conference represented "a cohort of younger scholars that could be harnessed to work together."[54] However, in October of 1979, Hatch and Noll, in consultation with George Marsden, presented a "Proposal to the Billy Graham Center for a Center for the Study of American Evangelicalism" that they had prepared the previous Spring.[55] The inspiration for the ISAE may have come from Hatch's and Noll's familiarity with Notre Dame's Cushwa Center for American Catholicism run by Catholic historian Jay Dolan.[56]

They based their proposal on the need they saw for evangelicals to understand their own history and traditions. Understanding their history had the dual purpose of helping evangelicals avoid the same mistakes committed by those who had gone before while equipping them with the insights of their forebears. They felt that the BGC and Wheaton College provided the best location for such a center owing to their physical resources, constituency, money, and established commitment to evangelical Christianity. Hatch and Noll believed the benefits derived from a center for the study of evangelical history would be similar to the inspiration the Oxford Movement produced for high church Anglicans and the Parker Society's influence on the maturing of British evangelicals. The proposal listed the activities the center would promote including assistance in building the BGC archives, holding biannual conferences, encouraging publications, sponsoring a scholar in residence program, and supplementing Wheaton's undergraduate and graduate programs in American Christianity. They defined the personnel needed to staff the center, the funding to run the center, and presented a proposed budget for 1980-81 and 1981-82.[57]

This information suggest that the idea for the ISAE was conceived long before Robert Linn proposed the idea to Hatch in November of 1979. It would appear, however, that Robert Linn provided Hatch and Noll with an alternative means for gaining the funding needed to start the ISAE.

Their proposal presented to the BGC in October of 1979 indicates that their initial plan had been to seek funding through the BGC and Wheaton College. Once Linn showed interest in the idea of an institute they began pursuing the Lilly Foundation for a planning grant to launch the ISAE.

By the Spring of 1981 the future of the ISAE rested on success in two crucial areas. Noll and Hatch had to convince the Lilly Foundation to provide the planning grant, and they had to convince the BGC of the merits of their idea in order to gain space for the ISAE in the BGC.[58] In January of 1982 a proposal for the ISAE was prepared during an all day conference that included Hatch, Noll, Joel Carpenter (Trinity College), Ward Kriegbaum (academic Vice President at Wheaton), and BGC staff members William Shoemaker, Mel Lortentzen, and Ivan Fahs. Hatch and Noll drew up the final draft in March of 1982.[59]

The final proposal was similar to the one they prepared in 1979. The central objective stated the purpose of the ISAE as assisting evangelicals in gaining a better perspective on their own experiences while helping non-evangelicals to understand "the historical significance and contemporary role of evangelicals."[60] They outlined a program design that included conferences, colloquies, visiting scholars, summer seminars, and publications. They intended to use the planning grant to host a conference at Wheaton in the Spring of 1983 on "The Shaping of Evangelical Christianity in Modern America." A large percentage of the budget was dedicated to this conference because they felt that "the future of the Institute will stand or fall on the impressions made by the Conference."[61] They also planned one or more academic colloquies on "The History of Fundamentalism." While Noll was on leave as a visiting scholar for the 1982-83 academic year, Nathan Hatch was appointed director of the institute with the assistance of Carpenter and Marsden. The final budget was $38,000.00, with the conference accounting for almost one third of this amount.[62] In May of 1982 the Lilly Foundation gave its approval for a fourteen month planning grant.[63]

The next crucial area involved the participation of the BGC. As stated before, some evangelicals were uncomfortable with the 1979 conference, and it seems there was a sense that these same people would not welcome the ISAE's association with the BGC. Therefore a rationale was developed addressing how the ISAE would complement the purposes of the BGC. The rationale presented to the BGC closely resembled that sent to Lilly with small changes. The central objective was enlarged to include the sentiments expressed in the earlier version of the proposal Hatch and Noll planned to present to the BGC in 1979. It included the importance of historical research for self-understanding with supporting parallels from the role of the Oxford Movement and Parker Society, but it expanded those examples to include the benefits of studying Jonathan Edwards, Charles Finney, Charles Hodge, George Whitefield and D. L. Moody.[64]

A planning session was then arranged for November 5-6, 1982 at the Lisle/Naperville Hilton. Invitations were sent to a variety of historians, theologians, and administrators associated with the project including: Joel Carpenter, Richard Chase (President of Wheaton College), John Dellenback (President of Christian College Coalition), David E. Johnston (Senior Administrative Officer for the BGC), Kenneth Kantzer (Trinity Evangelical Divinity School), and George Newitt (Board of Trustees, Wheaton College). This planning conference was broken into two parts. Friday night was given to the purpose and rationale of the ISAE while Saturday morning covered implementation and future direction.[65] The outline for the meeting indicates that the discussion was essentially a commentary and response on the various points of the rationale and the proposal approved by the Lilly Foundation.

Five months after the conference on "Evangelical Christianity and Modern America, 1930-1980," the Lilly Foundation awarded the ISAE a three year comprehensive grant of $174,000.00.[66] This grant virtually assured the institute's survival until 1986. The BGC also agreed during this period to provide space for the ISAE as an affiliate agency, and, in September of 1983, Joel Carpenter accepted the position as director of the ISAE. Not everyone was excited to see the birth of this new institute. A pastor in the Wheaton area wrote,

> As a local pastor, I find it very revolting and disappointing to see your efforts for an Institute for the studies of Evangelicals without any mention or cooperation with the National Association of Evangelicals officed right here as well. It may be wise and even helpful for you to consider this as they have 42 years track record and stand as the credible association of evangelicals in this country. For this reason related to a tight community, please forgive my remaining anonymous. (Signed) One in the Body of Christ.[67]

One immediate benefit of the Lilly grant was the start of informal meetings at the Craigville Conference Center at Hyannis Port, Massachusetts. These meetings were modeled to some degree after a seminar in Maine attended by Nathan Hatch and Grant Wacker and run by Timothy Smith.[68] The first Craigville meeting occurred June 12-17, 1984. Joel Carpenter sent invitations to those who would participate and encouraged them to bring their families along. Some of those who attended this first meeting included Nathan Hatch, James Hunter, Grant Wacker, Steve Marini, George Marsden, Mark Noll, Harry Stout, Timothy Smith and Joel Carpenter. These men were asked to bring portions of their latest work, and ideas for future projects in order to enter into a time of informal discussion.[69]

Mark Noll recalled that first meeting at Craigville as being both informal and productive. Randall Balmer shared the first chapter of what would eventually become a movie and book on the evangelical subculture, and Robert Linn was instrumental in getting a grant officer of the J. Howard Pew Freedom Trust to attend that first meeting and subsequent meetings.[70] He must have liked what he saw because in October of 1985 the J. Howard Pew Freedom Trust provided the ISAE with a three year grant worth $271,000.00.[71]

George Marsden remembered the meetings at Craigville being congenial because there was no real agenda other than what to do next. One idea that emerged from these informal meetings was the Evangelical Scholars Program which was funded by the Pew Trust and located in the Hesburgh Library at Notre Dame. This program networked scholars interested in evangelical concerns and helped channel resources to assist them with specific research projects. These meetings also introduced new people to the group like George Rawlyk, a Canadian historian from Queens University in Kingston, Ontario. Marsden singled out Hatch and Noll as the leaders in these meetings. "They think big ideas and implement them. They are seeking to promote broad Christian scholarship. Mark does a good bit of this informal networking constantly sending out stuff and writing, which helps build this network of interests and relationships."[72]

Nathan Hatch recalled the importance of the personal relationships formed at these meetings. Much of what happened was not designed but the atmosphere provided a means for interaction and good things resulted. Mark Noll encouraged Harry Stout to do his book on George Whitefield. The result was Stout's book, *The Divine Dramatist: George Whitefield and the Rise of Modern Evangelicalism*.[73] Hatch called those times at Craigville "a rare oasis." He also recognized that this network of scholar/ friends that grew from these meetings was sometimes misunderstood.

> I think sometimes this group takes flack from several fronts because we do hang out together. People in the field of church history overdo how much power and influence (we have). I'm sensitive to that as one could see that we are trying to manipulate something which I do not think is the case, but we run the risk of that because in the absence

of other blocks we are a sort of decided block, and not an inconsequential one when you consider the people involved. It's a fairly talented set of characters. I can't speak to myself but if you look at Wacker, Noll, and Marsden. I think it has one other not inconsequential development. It is the same cast of characters that have thought a lot about Christian scholarship.[74]

Mark Noll summarized his feelings about the network of friends, meetings and projects that surrounded the ISAE in the following way.

No one wrote this up as an intentional thing. It is providential, but I'm a Calvinist and everything is providential, but special I don't know. I never prayed directly that so and so would come to a meeting or conference, but I have prayed that my life would be meaningful for God. This whole operation has been a cause for me to thank the Lord for his goodness. This is far and away the most meaningful thing in my life outside of family and the local church. I would be a miserable person if I had known there was this thing and I would have missed it.[75]

The Craigville Conference Center was used every year from 1983 to 1992 for these informal but significant meetings. In 1993 the meetings were shifted to Stowe, Vermont in order to provide more space for the rapidly growing group of scholars and their families who attended. These meetings served the invaluable purpose of providing a means for linking together scholars of similar sympathies, interests, and concerns. The ISAE then served as an outlet for the intentional and unintentional ideas and projects that emerged from these times of discussion. Also, ideas for participants in the ISAE's many conferences often came from these meetings.

Beginning in 1983 the ISAE sponsored a steady stream of conferences funded by the Lilly Foundation and the Pew Trust. All these conferences, except one, were held at the BGC on the Wheaton campus. These conferences are listed by the year in which they occurred: "Jonathan Edwards and the American Experience" October 1984, "The Task of Evangelical Higher Education" May 1985, "A Century of World Evangelization" June 1986, and "A New Agenda for Evangelical Thought" June 1987.[76]

In 1988 there were three conferences assisted by a $63,000.00 planning grant from the Lilly Foundation and a $225,000.00 special grant from the Pew Trust. These conferences focused on the emerging role of the evangelical community in America and addressed the historical concerns and the present challenges they faced. The first two conferences were on "Religion and American Politics" in March of 1988 and "Evangelicals, the Mass Media, and American Culture" in September of 1988. The third conference was broken into two parts and entitled, "To Serve the Present Age."[77] This conference was held in Philadelphia, where the Pew Trust is based, and Paul Trimble of the Pew Trusts gave the greeting and invocation.[78] This conference was an indicator of the ISAE's commitment to engaging scholarship across a broad spectrum. Participants in this conference included a pastor from a charismatic church, an executive secretary of the National Council of Churches, a professor from Southern Methodist University, one from Holy Cross, one from UC Berkeley, the director of a Jewish study center, and a founder of the National Political Congress of Black Women. Recent conferences have included "Modern Christian Revivalism" April 1989, "Women in Evangelical History" May 1993, and "Theological Education in the Evangelical Tradition" December 1993.[79]

In addition to conferences, the ISAE enlarged its horizon to include other related projects. Books were published from the compiled and edited papers presented at the conferences. To date thirteen such books have been published. The ISAE also sponsored courses, colloquia, and public lectures on a variety of topics. In 1984, the ISAE, in cooperation with the History Department of Wheaton College, started a one year Masters program in American Church History. The network of evangelical historians associated with the ISAE comprised the faculty for this program. The ISAE provided the initial funding for Eerdman's *Library of Religious Biography* which included books on Billy Sunday, Roger Williams, George Whitefield, William Ewart Gladstone, and Aimee Semple McPherson. In 1983 the ISAE published its first edition of "The Evangelical Studies Bulletin." The bulletin is essentially an information piece with a scholarly slant. It includes a review essay, a bibliographic essay, news of interest to scholars, a list of monographs in the field, and a calendar of upcoming events.[80]

In the fourteen years since its inception the ISAE has become a significant part of the influence these Reformed evangelical historians exert in the field of American Christianity. If influence can be measured by funding, number of conferences, published books, and conference participants in terms of both their affiliations and locations, then the ISAE represents an influential organization. The ISAE has received in excess of two and a half million dollars, sponsored fourteen conferences, published thirteen separate volumes, and involved over 250 participants representing more than 100 affiliations and five continents.

Influence does not, however, always engender positive responses. With the passage of time, the ISAE continued to be a question mark in the minds of some evangelicals who felt that the Reformed historians associated with it were giving up their evangelical distinctives in exchange for academic respectability. Nathan Hatch commented that the ISAE had been criticized for its openness. "When we have a conference we invite the best people. There are some people at Trinity who didn't like that. At Trinity there are some who consider ISAE historians dangerous. They want to define evangelicalism doctrinally; if you don't believe in inerrancy you're not an evangelical."[81]

These historians perceived that their evangelical colleagues were suspicious of projects and institutes designed to be essentially intellectual. This perception was strengthened in 1987 when questions were raised about the appropriateness of the ISAE's affiliation with the BGC. Though these questions were present from the beginning and warranted a rationale on the appropriateness of their affiliation, there is reason to believe that the rationale to which the BGC agreed in 1982 was not the final word.

The main questions came via the Billy Graham Evangelistic Association's (BGEA) board through the staff of the BGC. It seems that the BGEA board wanted to separate the ISAE from the BGC. They had three reasons for this decision. First, they believed that the historians of the ISAE represented a position to the left of the BGEA's position on the Bible's inspiration, the Church's missionary task, and the relationship between religion and science. Next, they felt that the ISAE's parameters of discussion were too broad and allowed to many different beliefs which were, in the BGEA's view, confusing. They were concerned that these views and the books published from the conferences would be associated with Billy Graham. Finally, the BGEA board envisioned the BGC as a place where practical mission and ministry related skills would be developed. The ISAE was more of a think-tank which showed no immediate influence on evangelistic concerns.[82]

The BGC staff sought a compromise that would allow the ISAE to remain in the BGC but would turn its supplemental funding and affiliation over to Wheaton College. This solution did not find favor in the eyes of Joel Carpenter, the ISAE director. He was not convinced that such a move would favor either the ISAE or the BGC, but he was sure that the faculty and administration of Wheaton would not take kindly to "having someone else's problem dumped on them as a 'great opportunity'."[83] He also believed there was a question of credibility. The ISAE had earned some respect for the BGC in the academic world and this move could jeopardize that respect. He felt, however, that it was a good idea for the ISAE to build closer ties with the college in the event an actual move was needed.[84] He also believed that pursuing closer ties with the college would require some diplomacy. The fact that two major foundations contributed large sums of money to the institute may have provided some leverage in their diplomacy. At any rate, the ISAE remained where it was, for the time being, and in June of 1988 Carpenter left to become the director of the Pew Charitable Trusts' program in religion.[85] But, by 1992-93, the ISAE had been "nudged out of the Billy Graham Center."[86] Though the ISAE remains active and maintains its space in the Billy Graham Center, it is no longer officially supported by or affiliated with the BGC.

The issues raised in this chapter indicate that Nathan Hatch, George Marsden, and Mark Noll are more than mere historians who write and teach history. They have a purpose that extends beyond the bounds of historical scholarship. They are committed to a view of Christianity that motivates them to engage both the intellectual infrastructure of the evangelical community and the broader world of the American university. At first glance one is inclined to view their possible influence on these two communities as minimal, but, upon a closer look, the mounting evidence suggest that they have built a home for themselves in both camps that has the appearance of a weathered but permanent structure. They designed their home carefully, paying close attention to details like timing and the quality of their materials. As builders, they are perfectionists. They follow the maxims that there is strength in numbers and safety in a multitude of counselors. They draw on other scholars of like mind to ask the questions of "what if" and "why not?" They gather resources, provide motivation and assist others to implement their ideas. There is no magic to this process unless careful strategy, rigorous scholarship, close friendships, and efficient organization can be considered magic. They are moderate, Reformed, evangelical historians, with an agenda. The final verdict on their influence is not yet in.

Notes

[1] George Marsden, "Can Christianity Regain a Voice in a University?," taken from a draft of this speech prepared for and delivered at a conference on Christian higher education held at Messiah College, Pennsylvania, in May of 1993.

[2] George Marsden, *The Secularization of the Academy* (New York: Oxford Press, 1992), 5-6.

[3] Alvin Plantinga and Nicholas Wolterstorff, eds. *Faith and Rationality: Reason and Belief in God* (Notre Dame: University of Notre Dame Press, 1983).

[4] Alasdair MacIntyre, *Three Rival Versions of Moral Enquiry: Encyclopaedia, Genealogy, and Tradition* (Notre Dame: University of Notre Dame Press, 1990).

[5] Ibid., 7.

[6] Ibid., 11.

[7] Ibid., 14.

[8] Ibid., 14-15.

[9] Ibid., 17-20.

[10] Ibid., 24.

[11] Ibid., 29.

[12] Ibid., 30-31.

[13] Ibid., 35.

[14] George Marsden, "Christian Schooling: Beyond the multiversity," *Christian Century*, 7 October, 1992, 875.

[15] Ibid.

[16] Ibid.

[17] George Marsden, "The Ambiguities of Academic Freedom," *Church History* 62 (June 1993): 228. This subject is discussed further in chapter 16 of his book, *The Soul of the American University: From Protestant Establishment to Established Nonbelief* (New York: Oxford Press, 1994), 292-312. Chapter 17 provides additional insight by examining Fundamentalism's role in the further entrenchment of academic freedom as a criteria of credibility in the university.

[18] Ibid., 231. See also Robert M. McIver, *Academic Freedom in Our Time* (New York: Columbia University Press, 1955).

[19] Marsden, "Academic Freedom", 233-34.

[20] Ibid., 235.

[21] Nathan Hatch, "Christian Thinking in a Time of Academic Turmoil," *The Southern Baptist Educator*, August 1992, 6.

[22] Ibid., 8. See also Richard Hofstadter, *Anti-Intellectualism in American Life* (New York: Random House, 1962), 135. Hofstadter described religious anti-intellectualism as a "Manichean Mentality." He also characterized evangelical Protestantism as the prime example of the American impulse toward intellectual repression.

[23] Ibid., 8.

[24] Ibid., 9-11.

[25] Nathan Hatch, "Notre Dame's Quiet Revolution," a bulletin published in 1992 by Notre Dame to underscore its commitment to graduate research.

[26] Marsden Interview, June 2, 1993.

[27] Frank Vanden Berg, *Abraham Kuyper* (Grand Rapids: Wm. B. Eerdmans Publishing Company, 1960), 107.

[28] Gary Scott Smith, *The Seeds of Secularization: Calvinism, Culture, and Pluralism in America, 1870-1915* (Grand Rapids: Christian University Press, 1985), 106-07. Also see James D. Bratt, "The Dutch Schools" in *Dutch Reformed Theology*, ed. David Wells (Grand Rapids: Baker Book House, 1989), 13-32.

[29] Ibid.

[30] Nathan Hatch, Interview #2, June 2, 1993.

[31] Hatch, "Notre Dame's Quiet Revolution," 16.

[32] George Marsden, "The State of Evangelical Christian Scholarship," *Christian Scholar's Review* 17 (June 1988): 348. See also Marsden's study of Fuller Seminary, *Reforming Fundamentalism* (Grand Rapids: Eerdmans Pub. Company, 1987).

[33] Ibid., 353.

[34] Ibid., 356.

[35] Ibid., 357.

[36] Mark A. Noll, "The Scandal of the Evangelical Mind," delivered as the McManis Installation Lecture, February 9, 1993 at Wheaton College, 5.

[37] Ibid., 2.

[38] Ibid., 3.

[39] Ibid., 6.

[40] Ibid., 13-14.

[41] Allan Bloom, *The Closing of the American Mind* (New York: Simon and Schuster, Inc., 1987).

[42] Marsden, "Can Christianity Regain a Voice," 3.

[43] Ibid., 3-7. See also Marsden's discussion in chapters 13 and 14 of *The Soul of the American University*, 219-266.

[44] Nathan Hatch, "Comments on George Keller," delivered at a conference on Christian higher education held at Messiah College, Pennsylvania, in May of 1993, 4-5.

[45] Ibid., 5.

[46] Ibid., 7-8.

[47] Ibid., 9-10.

[48] Mark Noll Interview, June 4, 1993.

[49] Ibid.

[50] Nathan O. Hatch and Mark A. Noll, eds. *The Bible in America* (New York: Oxford University Press, 1982). Martin Marty, in his review, referred to the historical judgements expressed in this book as sign of maturing evangelical scholarship. Martin E. Marty, review of *The Bible in America*, Nathan O. Hatch and Mark A. Noll, eds., in *The American Historical Review* 88 (June 1983): 745.

51 Information based on a ten year study done by the ISAE in the summer of 1993 and provided to me by that organization.

52 Noll Interview, June 4, 1993.

53 Information gathered from a copy of the conference brochure provided by Mark Noll, June 4, 1993.

54 Noll Interview, June 4, 1993.

55 Information on the proposal was obtained through Mark Noll as was the letter indicating Marsden's contribution, which was part of an interdepartmental correspondence between Noll and the staff of the BGC.

56 Joel Carpenter to Jay Dolan, October 13, 1983, files of the ISAE.

57 From "Proposal to the Billy Graham Center", prepared by Mark Noll and Nathan Hatch, October 1979. Provided by Mark Noll, June 4, 1993.

58 Mark Noll to Mel Lortentzen, January 27, 1982, files of the ISAE.

59 From the copy of a letter sent to Robert Linn by the BGC, files of the ISAE.

60 From copy of rationale given to BGC, provided by Mark Noll June 4, 1993.

61 Mark Noll to Mel Lortentzen, January 27, 1982, files of ISAE.

62 From copy of "Planning Grant" sent to the Lilly Endowment, March 1982, files of ISAE.

63 Information obtained ISAE study in summer of 1993.

64 Information obtained from a copy of the rationale provided by Mark Noll, June 4, 1993.

65 Form letter, Nathan Hatch to Colleague, October 28, 1982. Lists of participants and outline obtained from the files of the ISAE.

66 Joel Carpenter to Jay Dolan, October 13, 1982, files of the ISAE.

67 Obtained from the files of the ISAE, June 5, 1993.

68 Noll Interview, June 4, 1993.

69 Joel Carpenter to Robert Calhoon, November 11, 1983, and Joel Carpenter to Steve Marini, November 11, 1983, files of the ISAE.

70 Noll Interview, June 4, 1993.

71 Joel Carpenter to Timothy Smith, November 11, 1985, files of the ISAE.

72 Marsden Interview, June 2, 1993.

73 Harry S. Stout, *The Divine Dramatist: George Whitefield and the Rise of Modern Evangelicalism* (New Haven: Yale University Press, 1991).

74 Hatch Interview #2, June 2, 1993.

75 Noll Interview, June 4, 1993.

76 Information obtained from study done by ISAE. Books from these conferences included: Joel Carpenter and Kenneth Shipps, eds., *Making Higher Education Christian* (Grand Rapids: Eerdmans Publishing Company, 1988) and Nathan Hatch and Harry Stout, eds., *Jonathan Edwards and the American Experience* (New York: Oxford University Press, 1988). One review of this volume indicated that the way in which the information was selected was a possible drawback to the discussion. This assessment was based on the fact that the book reflected the views of participants in a conference who were not selected

because of their involvement in current Edwards research. William H. Brackney, review of *Jonathan Edwards and the American Experience*, Nathan Hatch and Harry Stout, eds., In *The Baptist Quarterly* (London) 33 (April 1990): 295.

[77] Ibid.

[78] Information obtained from brochure on conference provide by the ISAE.

[79] ISAE study.

[80] Ibid.

[81] Hatch Interview #2, June 2, 1993.

[82] Joel Carpenter to Nathan Hatch and Mark Noll, February 23, 1987, files of the ISAE.

[83] Ibid.

[84] Ibid.

[85] Joel Carpenter to Jim Kraakevik, December 19, 1988, files of the ISAE.

[86] Nathan Hatch, "Comments on George Keller," May 1993.

5

An Evangelical Mafia?

This book has examined the historical methodology, research content and academic goals of George Marsden, Nathan Hatch, and Mark Noll. These men were chosen because they represent a larger network of neoevangelical historians characterized by close friendships and cooperative academic efforts. It is this same network that Leonard Sweet referred to as "one of the most arresting phenomenon in American religious scholarship today."[1]

In the course of this study the personal backgrounds of these historians have also been examined. They were reared in conservative religious traditions and, with some variation, have remained among theological conservatives. They were educated in both sectarian and secular institutions and, though they have chosen to practice their historical professions in sectarian schools, they are indebted to secular graduate schools for their training in historical methodology. They have approached the evangelical academic world as the bearers of glad tidings. They announce that the time has come for evangelicals to cast off their anti-intellectual chains and confidently reenter the world of academic discourse. They are received with joy by those evangelical scholars who have waited for a champion to come and lead the way. Scholars outside the evangelical camp look on this new vanguard of neoevangelical historians with guarded optimism. Some of these scholars like what they hear and read, but ask where do these historians come from and what is their agenda; other scholars refer to these evangelical historians as the "evangelical mafia." Then there are those evangelicals who look on with suspicion. They do not like what they hear and read from this rising block of historians who call themselves evangelicals. These evangelicals predict that compromise is on the horizon. They are uncomfortable with these historians' openness in engaging the academic world outside of evangelicalism. They remember Fuller Seminary and the first neoevangelicals, and they do not welcome these new heirs of that heritage.

These new evangelical historians established the Institute for the Study of American Evangelicals as a mouthpiece for their historical research.

They organized it to serve as a resource for the historical study and understanding of evangelicalism and as a link with the academic community outside evangelicalism. Through conferences, colloquia, and historical publications the ISAE has successfully engaged both communities, but, in the process, it transgressed the established theological and cultural boundaries of its own community. As a result, the ISAE was cut off from the Billy Graham Center. It remains active and, for the moment, funded, but the ISAE and the historians it represents will not receive the endorsement of those who speak for the evangelical popular court.

The volatile combination of their evangelical faith and their historical methodology serves both as an identity and a dilemma for these historians. George Marsden, Nathan Hatch, and Mark Noll identify the Reformed aspect of the evangelical tradition as the basis for their confessional beliefs. Yet that identity serves as a dilemma when they write history. Their research alienates non-Reformed evangelicals, like Donald Dayton, who feel that Marsden, Hatch, and Noll slant their history to fit a Reformed understanding or paradigm, and they are criticized by both non-sectarian and sectarian historians who feel their research is too confessional.

All three of these historians are influenced by the Dutch Reformed tradition. This tradition has a shaping affect on the way they perceive the purpose of historical research and the emphasis they place on the life of the mind. This is not to say, however, that these men set out to consciously fit their research into some kind of Reformed mold or paradigm. The fact that their research is heavily slanted toward the more Reformed aspects of American Protestantism seems to be more a matter of personal preference in historical research rather than an attempt at being intentionally biased.

Although they show an awareness of general trends in research toward examining American forms of the Christian religion and recovering the history of groups that have in the past been marginalized, they choose to study primarily the contribution of evangelical Protestants to American Christianity. It is in this respect that their research and definitions seem somewhat narrow. One is sometimes left with the impression that when they refer to what is Christian in American history or to what represents a Christian worldview, they are actually referring to evangelical Christians. They are more careful to make distinctions in this regard when writing about America's political past, but are not so careful when referring to the struggle over finding a unified intellectual tradition for the modern American university. In this respect their references to a Christian worldview often seem to presuppose a Dutch Reformed or at least an evangelical worldview.

All three of these men sit close to the fence that marks the property line between faith and learning. They operate methodologically as any other historian in that they use critical methods of research. On the other hand, the nature of their historical interests in the contribution of evangelical Christianity to America poses a problem. The evangelical faith is by nature a confessional tradition. It is a tradition whose authority is based upon the revelation of the Bible, aided by reason. They write the history of this tradition as heirs of it and as participants in it, but attempt to do so as objective observers. They have gained a reputation for being overtly critical of those aspects of their tradition that have been anti-intellectual and culture denying, utilizing history as a corrective for these beliefs as they find expression in the evangelical community. But critiquing their tradition also allows them the freedom to commend it. Historians who are open about their confessional stance and are self-conscious about their method must remain alert to the danger of research that begins as a corrective and ends as a sermon. Critiquing one's own tradition can become a subtle apologetic for it.

The historical research of George Marsden, Nathan Hatch, and Mark Noll has been examined in light of their connection to and concern for the evangelical community. As a result, it is hoped that greater insight has been gained for understanding these men's aspirations and goals. Marsden, Hatch, and Noll all claim some form of evangelical/fundamentalist background. In terms of historical research and personal experiences they understand this tradition. They understand how this tradition is rooted in conservative social and religious views. These historians are the conscious heirs of the neoevangelical movement of the 40s and 50s and are progressives in their intellectual views; however, they primarily write and speak to grassroots evangelicals who remain captive to the religious and social ideals of fundamentalism. This regnant fundamentalism may seriously affects these historian's hopes of influencing the evangelical community to take seriously the life of the mind.

These scholars are dedicated to clarifying, instructing, and/or correcting various deficiencies in the evangelical community's understanding of the role of scholarship. But when they turn from the technical field of historical research to enter the practical discussion surrounding the actual state of evangelical higher education, their findings frustrate them. They discover an evangelical philosophy of education that acknowledges a role for academics without recognizing the need to intellectually or financially compete with the leading universities in

America. This is a disturbing trend for these men who see as their ultimate goal the changing of this evangelical philosophy of education. Their efforts at changing this prevailing philosophy may be hampered by several factors. The suspicion felt by some evangelicals regarding intellectual change often fosters an environment of distrust. These historians can alienate themselves from the evangelical academic community if they push their desired changes too quickly without first gaining strong support from within evangelical institutions. In addition their influence on evangelical academic life may depend on their professional investment in evangelical institutions of learning.

Of the three men, only Mark Noll of Wheaton College holds a faculty position at an evangelical institution. In a lecture given at Wheaton, he called the evangelical lack of commitment to education scandalous. Referring to this lack of intellectual commitment, he accused some evangelicals of being gnostics, docetists, and Manicheans. In other words, he believed they were intellectual heretics. Noll does not support the Enlightenment principles upon which the modern university is founded but he chastises his own tradition for not having the modern university's commitment to scholarly excellence. He may find it difficult to have it both ways. Evangelicals have not traditionally emphasized scholarship and they have been inclined to view their faith in revivalistic terms rather than as an intellectual alternative to the Enlightenment. While Noll acknowledges that the recent history of evangelicalism has not been one of intellectual commitment, he remains hopeful that this history can be change.

Marsden and Hatch do not hold faculty positions at an evangelical institution. Though Hatch is a trustee of Wheaton College, both he and Marsden teach at Notre Dame. They urge evangelicals to be committed to the cost of intellectual excellence in higher education, but do so from within the confines of the Roman Catholic confessional tradition. They enjoy the best of both worlds at Notre Dame in that they can operate freely as evangelical Christian scholars while being supported by the money and resources of the Roman Catholic Church. They benefit from Notre Dame's dedication to a level of scholarship and graduate research that is not possible within the evangelical community where financial resources are dispersed among so many smaller institutions. The fact that they hold positions at a Roman Catholic university may ultimately affect the amount of influence they will exert on evangelical academic life. Though they feel comfortable at Notre Dame because the Roman Catholic intellectual tradition is similar to their own Dutch Calvinism, they must know that Dutch Calvinism, for all its intellectual influence, remains a small cultural enclave in the wider world of evangelicalism.

All three men, at some time in their education, benefited from the secular university system. They understand the requirements of a deep commitment to intellectual excellence. What they see as the evangelical community's abandonment of intellectual excellence concerns these historians. The problem these men face is that they want to influence the educational philosophy of a diverse and often divisive tradition that lacks a strong, continuous intellectual tradition. Their own commitment to the importance of scholarship among evangelical Christians has produced a prodigious amount of rigorous scholarship. Their scholarship has enriched and challenged not only their own community, but many in the broader historical guild as well. What they have accomplished and continue to accomplish in historical scholarship sets these three men and their other evangelical colleagues apart as a significant school of evangelical historians. Their research will continue to make a significant contribution to the understanding of evangelical Christianity in America, but they are, to some degree, isolated in their influence. Their historical and educational views are not fully accepted among those evangelicals they wish to influence, and, though they are respected by those in the historical guild, their confessional position, small numbers, and lack of institutional authority, may limit their influence.

George Marsden, Nathan Hatch, and Mark Noll are Reformed evangelical historians with an academic and historical agenda. They view their role as historians as both a profession and a calling. They take seriously the Dutch Reformed perspective that one's profession is an opportunity to honor God with life and vocation. They therefore pursue the study of history as a way to be true to their Christian commitment and with the hope of persuading others in the evangelical community to take seriously the life of the mind. They have reasserted the value and place of religious ideas as a significant force in the interpretation of American history. Likewise, they have participated in the contemporary discussion over the value of religious thought in the mission of the modern university. In the process, Marsden, Hatch, and Noll have engaged the wider academic world where they hope to leave a lasting contribution. Of these hopes Mark Noll said:

> I have no delusions we will change the historical profession. We have had a drop in the bucket effect. It's been a real drop, but certainly not a bombshell. I think it will be a legacy but not a grandiose one. It will not turn everything around. If we all died today there would

be something left, but it would be modest. I think what we have done will help some people, not as a indelible blueprint but hopefully as a pointer, a suggestion of how to go.[2]

As the leaders of an emerging evangelical school of historical thought, George Marsden, Nathan Hatch, and Mark Noll have helped shape a historical alternative for evangelical research, one that combines confessional commitment with rigorous scholarship. It is not a yet legacy but it is already a pointer, a suggestion to future evangelical historians of how to go.

Notes

1 Leonard I. Sweet, "Wise as Serpents, Gentle as Doves: The New Evangelical Historiography," *Journal of the American Academy of Religion* 56 (Fall 1988): 397.

2 Mark Noll Interview, June 4, 1993.

Index